On Silbury Hill

ADAM THORPE

A LITTLE TOLLER MONOGRAPH

Published by Little Toller Books in 2014

Little Toller Books, Lower Dairy, Toller Fratrum, Dorset DT2 0EL

Typeset in Monotype Garamond and Perpetua by Little Toller Books

Printed by TJ International, Padstow, Cornwall

All papers used by Little Toller Books are natural, recyclable products
made from wood grown in sustainable, well-managed forests

A catalogue record for this book is available from the British Library

ISBN 978-1-908213-24-2

To all those who built her; to everything that grows on her

Neither gentleman had ever seen Avebury, but Dr. Martineau had once visited Stonehenge.

'Avebury is much the oldest,' said the doctor. 'They must have made Silbury Hill long before 2000 B.C. It may be five thousand years old or even more. It is the most important historical relic in the British Isles. And the most neglected.'

They exchanged archaeological facts. The secret places of the heart rested until the afternoon.

H.G. Wells, *The Secret Places of the Heart* (1922)

One

The point about Silbury Hill is that she has no point.

She has been described as 'standing in the Kennet meadows like a grassed-over coal tip'. A sudden doubter, I spent an hour on the web searching for images of abandoned spoil tips. None of them resembled Silbury. They were either disguised by conifers or looked messy, the result of what W.B. Yeats called, in his poem 'Meru', man's 'ravaging, ravening and uprooting'.

Spoil heaps, even when colonised by tough and thorny stuff, look like spoil heaps: there is no thought in them, only convenience, and they are ugly. They have a point, they are practical, as any mound of waste is practical. Silbury Hill looks as much like a grassed-over coal tip as the Roman forum looks like an abandoned building site.

Silbury is the more beautiful for being almost ugly. I have known her since the age of thirteen.

If anything, she resembles what archaeologists call a 'tell', from the Hebrew and Arabic for hillock: a mound created from centuries of disintegrating mud-brick houses and the detritus of urban life, accreting generation after generation in the dry lands of the Middle East. The tell under Baalbeck's Temple of Jupiter in Lebanon contains 9,000 years of continuous settlement. Except that Silbury's accretions are deliberate and ungraspable, the expression of an urge or a need that we cannot decipher.

Not very forthcoming, as my mother used to say about someone shy or diffident.

She may not be forthcoming, but she is very large and imposing: the largest man-made hill in Europe, and only beaten elsewhere by the Tomb of Alyattes near Sardis in Turkey (260 feet high, with a circumference of three-quarters of a mile), built in the seventh century BC and nestling among nearly 100 other burial mounds – the royal necropolis of Lydia. Silbury is not a burial mound. Constructing something of this size out of soil and stony rubble without it collapsing is in itself an achievement. In this case, we have a mound that has lasted virtually intact for thousands of years.

Furthermore, she was constructed without earth-movers or diggers, without power tools, without iron tools, without rulers and surveying instruments and hard hats, with only antler picks and ox shoulder blades and wickerwork baskets, plus human muscle. At around 130 feet high, she is equivalent to a thirteen-storey building. If the *Titanic* sailed just behind her in your dreams, you would only see the smoke from the funnels. If the Statue of Liberty could be placed likewise, only the bronze flame of the torch would poke above the flattish summit.

Her base covers five acres of Wiltshire turf, the equivalent of three football pitches. Five acres that have not seen sunlight or stars for some 4,300 years and will never see sunlight again until, possibly, the ice of the next Ice Age to extend as far as southern England scratches her away like a pimple.

In her day she must have been almost unimaginably

colossal, since nothing else man-made came anywhere near. She was probably as white, when completed, as the dome of the Taj Mahal – not with marble, but with ungrassed chalk. To visitors seeing her for the first time, she would have seemed otherworldly, miraculous, impossibly smooth and symmetrical: like a vast upturned bowl. It is probable that the scooped-out ditch left around her by the construction was naturally flooded, like a moat, giving her a mirroring surround.

Oddly – almost incredibly given our surfeited imagination, our seen-it-all consciousness, our overloaded Dubai-busy cortex – her heap of grassy chalk still seems otherworldly. She rears up quite abruptly as you drive westward on the A4 (or 'the Bath Road') from Marlborough, slightly sunken beyond the spur that the road has followed for at least 2,000 years, and always surprising.

Yet without someone standing at her base or (now forbidden) on top of her to give us a comparison, her scale grows blurred. From the viewing area by the little car park under the trees, or from the nearby footpath to the north-west that leads to the Avebury stone circle, or from the Kennet stream the other side of the Bath Road, she seems almost too small, almost a grassy knoll. A giant knoll, but still a knoll.

Walk the path towards Waden Hill, then climb until you can look across and down at her; not too far, or the crest of the hill begins to swallow her up. And what happens?

She grows into something gigantic.

Is it just me, or does she seem to be expanding, swelling, like a speeded-up pregnancy?

And I'm not even persuaded by the Great Goddess theory, or no more than by all the other theories. Deep in the 1970s, I read Michael Dames's book *The Silbury Treasure*, purchased in Watkins Books, the ambrosial esoteric bookshop in London's Cecil Court. I was seduced. The author gives the impression that he has unlocked something, doing it so well and evocatively that even if you doubt his explanation, you want him to be right. His diagrams, evoking parallel images of ancient 'Venus' figurines, of a great all-seeing eyeball or a pregnant belly, make it seem blatantly obvious that Silbury is a massive sculpture of Mother Earth nearly at her term, a gigantic harvest hill gouged and heaped from the low-lying terrain as an honouring of the soil's natural fertility. As I had always seen Silbury as 'her', the seduction was swift.

The bulk of Dames's theory rests on the fragile wings of a certain species of flying ant, discovered in the turf base during the most famous of the several archaeological probings (Professor Richard Atkinson's in 1968), and suggesting that the project began in early August at harvest-time, when such ants briefly grow wings. Except that the flying ants were not found: or at least, no report or physical evidence of their remains has been produced.

A shame. We may live, as Lorca put it, 'mired in numbers and laws,/In mindless games, in fruitless labours', but something about Silbury's painstaking, back-breaking labour feels full of fruitfulness, even though we have no idea what that was. For Charles Knight, writing in the highly utilitarian 1840s, when Avebury and Stonehenge were 'Druidic temples', she had to be a kind of Albert Memorial:

> The great earthworks of a modern railway are the results of labour, assisted by science and stimulated by capital, employing itself for profit; but Silbury Hill in all likelihood was a gigantic effort of what has been called hero-worship, a labour for no direct or immediate utility, but to preserve the memory of some ruler, or lawgiver, or warrior, or priest.

The accompanying etching in *Old England* shows a thoroughly utilitarian haywain creaking along the rutted Bath Road in front of the Hill. The haywain itself now belongs to another world, of course: 'Old England' indeed.

Silbury Hill, in Wiltshire,—Conjectured to be a sepulcral Barrow.

Silbury's stillness is like the exaggerated stillness after much noise. Her lost noise, and our present din. We flicker and zip around her, like a speeded-up film that squashes years into minutes, and she stays quietly the same, giving nothing away.

Not that we haven't tried to change her: after weeks of heavy rain, a large hole appeared on her summit at the beginning of our own millennium, the vestige of a vertical shaft dug by miners supervised by Edward Drax in 1776 – the first of three major insults to her body over the next 200 years: in the mid-nineteenth century Dean Merewether dug in from the side and Richard Atkinson followed suit in the 1960s, filmed by the BBC. Each was a bid to reveal her mystery, to give bone to the local legend of King Sil lying in his gold at her core, still mounted. Given the cumulative effect of these tunnels and voids, she was considered in danger of collapse. I thought: if Silbury collapses, so will I. Psychologically, anyway. This is probably unhealthy. To be so dependent for your sanity on a great prehistoric lump of chalky earth!

The hill did not collapse: by May 2008, the hole and tunnels had been filled in with 500,000 pounds of crushed and liquified chalk, sealing her for good, and Silbury now looks better than ever, partly because no one is allowed to climb her, let alone to dig into her. The scars of many puffing visitors are pretty well healed: there is no longer a chalk-white, foot-battered walk-up. Our contemplation of her is not spoilt by little figures in blotches of bright rainwear or solecisms of summery shorts labouring up the slopes, their kids squealing distantly, their dogs doing that idiotic barking thing, the final summit and the sky measuring them off into tiny iron filings moved about by some giant magnet pressing beneath. She is no longer a tripper's plaything, scattered with sweet wrappers and cellophane, a free place to roll down if you don't mind the sheep shit. She is sacred again. She is not to be approached.

She has, in fact, been designated a Site of Special Scientific Interest – mainly because of her flowers, and particularly for the resident population of the rare knapweed broomrape: flowering on a tall, thick stem that tapers towards the bottom, it resembles a giant pipe cleaner or what sax players call a 'shove-it': parasitic on the blue thistle-like greater knapweed, lacking chlorophyll, it has no green leaves and its flowers are a rusty purple-brown. Now it can flourish untrampled on the slopes of its equally weird hill.

Glory be to God, declared Gerard Manley Hopkins, for 'All things counter, original, spare, strange'. Such things have their work cut out, these days. Praise be to all strange things that don't fit the cut, and to the great strangeness that is Silbury.

She is not, of course, without prehistoric companions on the downs of Wiltshire and Berkshire. There is a very funny episode, entitled *Silbury Hill*, of the French cult comedy series *Kaamelott*, in which Arthur accuses Guinevere and his mother-in-law of trespassing on yet another sacred site after they had picknicked on '*la colline de Silbury*'. His mother-in-law retorts that, in Arthur's village, you can't move three steps without stumbling on a 'magic site'. That is still true now, and it must have been truer thousands of years ago. But tumuli and stone circles and long barrows, while impressive, are simply not as, well, quirky-looking.

Contemplated from the signboard, controlled, she may yet become simply picturesque, a whimsical kink in the peaceful landscape. Hands off, this is a Site of Special Scientific Interest, thanks not only to her flora but to her grassland birds and butterflies – including corn buntings and marbled whites. This is a Classified Monument of International Significance, thanks to her age. This is the tended property of English Heritage, thanks to them stumping up the money to save her. The terrible day might come when hidden security cameras are installed, connected to the police station in Marlborough or Devizes, to catch those climbing her. Perhaps they already are. We might rage on blogs, but it will all be done for the Hill's benefit.

In Roman times there were Roman temples and shrines dotting her slopes, and a large, now-vanished settlement with villas pooled around her base where there are now fields: not just the ancient equivalent of a motorway service station on the Bath to London highway, we assume. Appropriation by the gods, no doubt a money-spinner, shrouds of incense, but a recognition of a powerful place that was already (although they didn't know it) 2,300 years old. Some kind of veneration, certainly. No Roman tunnel having been found, we know that those skilled miners of lead never sought treasure inside her, either out of respect or fear (they also left their own barrows mottling the landscape), or because they knew she was never a mausoleum. So what did those hard-eyed folk make of this inverted cooking bowl, rearing by their efficient road so that its straight progress had to deviate? What rules did they apply?

Certainly not those that arise from a purely pragmatic objectivity, a scientific and environmental assessment that detaches and boxes and fences and plonks a warning notice just in case, legally, we plead ignorance. Well, the no-nonsense Saxons put a hillfort on the top using massive wooden posts, so we're in good company.

Silbury has gone global, that's the thing. She is no longer properly local.

For hundreds of years, post-pagan Silbury was berthed in the lives of the people who lived around her. The evidence is sparse, but we have it: a fun place to climb, to look at the view, to take your lover to, or simply as a matter-of-fact, familiar presence, part of the background hum – until Palm Sunday, when you could join the ritual merry-making on the top involving water from the River Kennet's spring the other side of the road, along with figs and cakes. This went on well into the nineteenth century, the faintest anthropological echo of Neolithic belief. Or, as Dames puts it, 'Silbury … finally died, as a stage for communal behaviour, in the nineteenth century AD … the long veneration was finished.'

It is astonishing that she can no longer be climbed, in fact: when at school at Marlborough College five miles up the road, and later when living on the downs, I climbed Silbury many times myself, and on a few occasions since. I have a flickery, silent Super-8 film from the 1970s of my maxi-skirted sister scrambling up with a friend in what looks like a stiff breeze. I have been estranged from her (and therefore my young nephew and niece) for many years, and so watching it makes me think about kith and kin in a melancholy way.

What does it mean to belong? What does it mean to be of the same blood? What does England mean to me now I see so little of my family on these islands beyond our own grown-up children?

Silbury can be very personal with her questions.

These days, this hill of memories is a fragile museum exhibit: all she lacks is a glass case. Gone are the times when fingers closed on her tussocks, the giggling downland lass struggling up with her pimply courting lad – who wonders whether to give her a hand and then does so, feeling the softness of her palm with its farmworking callouses against his own dry roughness, the bodily weight of her jerky tug which is something extraordinary and then, as he slips over on a smear of sheep droppings, the same weight bundling past as if she has turned into laughing air just yards from the summit, and him cursing happily because he is so happy when all's right with the world, despite his right mitten being in a stink of clot.

A pastoral scene that happened, thousands of times over, and will happen no more. The loss is part of a much broader loss, a loss of communal innocence and belonging. After all, the greatest damage to Silbury was done by antiquarians, the pokings of early archaeologists – Edward Drax's shaft in 1776, Henry Blandford's and John Merewether's deep tunnellings of 1849, Alfred Pass's and Flinders Petrie's shallow trenches in 1886 and 1922 respectively, with Richard Atkinson boring another access tunnel and drilling a series of cores in 1968 – live in front of the BBC cameras. Oh, and by outside visitors arriving in their carriages and cars, scoring the sides with their scrabblings.

Yet let's not be sentimental about this, either: I doubt just anyone would have been allowed to climb Silbury when she was sacred in whatever way she was sacred. Now she is sacred in a very downbeat, sensible, twenty-first century way: a scientific and secular way. And even museum exhibits can be potent. My wife's Polish-Jewish uncle-by-marriage, the only survivor in his family of the Holocaust, a Zen potter and painter, would visit the British Museum every week to draw inspiration and comfort from just six exhibits. Potency resides within the object: we connect – and draw the current.

And it was, I'm afraid, the locals – certain of them, those

who would gain, who had already gained – who destroyed the great stone circles nearby and flattened the tumuli. It was locals who relished the café and garage erected yards from Silbury on the A4 in the 1920s, to the protests of the experts. There is a photograph of it, dating from the 1930s – Auden's 'low, dishonest decade': the Hill looks squat and grey behind the pumps, the rooves of corrugated iron, the clipped hedge, the wooden posts, the signs for refreshments. She looks, in fact, like a coal tip.

If only one in ten locals sees an opening and is minded to draw the profit, or smash what conjures their own fettered inadequacy, claustrophobia and frustration, then that is more than enough to justify outside intervention, to impose rules, to establish limits, to shut the window.

Remember the Lascaux caves.

I arrived as a boy just a fortnight after they had been closed off as an emergency measure in 1963, the painted limestone walls tattered green by bacterial and algal infection. Bewildered crowds stood about in the gusts of pine-sweetened heat, denied the experience of a lifetime.

News was slower to travel back then. My disappointment was almost as profound as my parents'. It was locals who, in the autumn of 1940, had leapt into business days after the discovery of the caves by the village boys, erecting a sign that said "Grotte de Lascaux – 2 kilometres" until, twenty years later, the site was receiving 1,500 visitors a day. And if it hadn't been locals, it would have been some other sharp-eyed exploiter of an opportunity.

Sometimes it isn't a question of exploiting but surviving, as around the pyramids of Egypt in our own day. When in 1770 William Gilpin visited the picturesque ruins of Tintern Abbey, shortly to be memorialised by Wordsworth, he found a hamlet of little huts inhabited by beggars and would-be guides whose 'poverty and wretchedness ... were remarkable'. They included a paralysed woman shuffling along on sticks who showed them the so-called monks' library – her own home, in fact, trickling with 'chilling damps': a horrified Gilpin confesses that he had never seen 'so loathsome a human dwelling'.

Whether through desperate need or no, the ability to see an opening is what distinguished modern humans from the Neanderthal, whose tools remained numbingly unchanged for 200,000 years, despite climatic changes including harsh cold. Which doesn't explain why, around 2400 BC, a bunch of Neolithic locals (we assume!) decided to expend an estimated 18 million man-hours on heaping up 250,000 cubic metres of chalk over a probable minimum period of a hundred years, for no good reason that we can discern.

Two

Silbury's strangeness is not just conceptual, but aesthetic. Chalk downland proceeds like the sea seen from a gently rolling ship: intersecting waves, mild billows, a long horizon. A scarp is the most dramatic element in downland, a sometimes quite steep slope where the layer of sedimental rock called Upper Greensand has nudged up through the younger chalk. The northernmost scarp, along which the ancient track called the Ridgeway runs, provides a kind of boundary for the North Wessex Downs – a modern name that draws on Alfred the Great's kingdom for its antique credentials. The South Downs take the springy turf down to the Channel, to climb out of the sea again in France – which is why, after a brief training on Salisbury Plain and a night boat and train to Picardy, the downland labourer enlisted for the trenches alighted and looked about him and thought the whole world was like home, apart from the booms of guns.

Aside from scarps (the word itself conjuring their scooped and cresting feel), the landscape here doesn't do verticals. The land stays low and rolling and yet, as W.H. Hudson observed, 'we feel on top of the world'. The sky is almost as enormous as Norfolk's. On the downs, however, the land never stops inflating itself here and there, like a quietly breathing dragon stretched out as far as the eye can see. This is not really flatness at all, but a continuously curving and interleaving set of planes with very shallow arcs. Copses tuft these and stand out darkly against the sky, except on stormy or windy days when they might momentarily snarl the sun and turn as bright as polished gold against the dark bruise of the clouds.

But then, at a certain slow bend on the A4, Silbury happens. She emulates a hill, not even a miniature hill but a grown-up one: she seems natural – her slope is close to what is known as the normal 'angle of repose' for settling chalk – but at the same time impossible because hills like that do not belong here.

Somewhere, just possibly, she might have suited: here where I live in the Cévennes mountains, I have seen many Silbury-shaped hills nestling happily among their sisters, great and small. Even in the rolling curves of the Auvergne, surrounded by that area's grassed-over volcanic cones that erupt silently and almost artificially from the great green swards, she would have felt at home; more so among Iceland's still active peaks, coming in all sizes but their shapes so volcano-like they resemble a child's drawing. And look, there she is in the Pyrenees, nestling modestly at the foot of glacially-twisted heights, just another (minor) feature to admire as you haul your big-booted self along some beetling crest.

But there are, it has to be admitted, two natural formations in the area that eerily remind us of our artificial alp.

A few miles north-east and located just below the ancient chalk cut-out known as the Uffington White Horse, Dragon

Hill resembles a miniature Silbury (it's a quarter of the size) with flanks ridged like the sinews of a taut neck; but only its deliberately levelled top is not natural. The rest is grassed-over calcareous outcrop near the bottom of White Horse Hill's sweeping, muscular scarp. Possible echoes of some ritual use survive in the legend that St George killed the dragon on the eponymous tump, the toxic blood scorching a permanently bald spot on its crown. This whole place, occult energies aside, has a pronounced aesthetic charge in its windswept lines and forms: the white horse gallops in a magnificent context, and Dragon Hill fits.

Silbury, however, fits nothing. She not only looks startlingly eccentric, she looks radical in the disturbing way favoured by modernism: surreal, or nudging towards pure form. And this is why recent artists from Paul Nash to David Inshaw have been so attracted to her. 'Prehistory,'

notes Alexandra Harris in *Romantic Moderns*, her analysis of the English arts between the wars, 'had an impressive list of modern advocates appropriating its monuments for their various visions of England.'

Silbury certainly prompts contradictions. The early field archaeologist and antiquarian William Stukeley, to whose pioneering work we owe so much of our knowledge of Avebury and Stonehenge, drew the hill in 1723. A doctor, he was trained to record accurately: thanks to his *Itinerarium Curiosum*, an illustrated record of his travels, we have a better idea of what pre-industral Britain looked like – or rather, of what we have lost. John Piper has memorably commented: 'To jump, run, walk, or struggle up each slope with Stukeley in his drawing is as real and as sharp an experience as to take a journey round a wineglass with Picasso.'

Stukeley's knowledge of chalk country (as well as of prehistoric sites) was deep and intimate: particularly striking in his drawing is the deeply sunken and rutted nature of the Bath Road, equally visible in a wonderful roadside etching of the hill by the Wiltshire antiquarian Richard Colt Hoare (1758–1838), where the overgrown banks are at least 10 feet high. But Stukeley's curves and shadows and dots of trees lead our eye on a purely sensual journey of plane and form that undercuts the image's topographical, even anatomical, nature. There is, Piper notes, something very contemporary in the interplay of these two atmospheres. It seems to anticipate the paintings of Paul Nash, those that juxtapose a downland landscape with hard-edged, geometric forms planted among the combes like alien monoliths or school maths exercises.

Henry Moore's monolithic sculptures are anything but

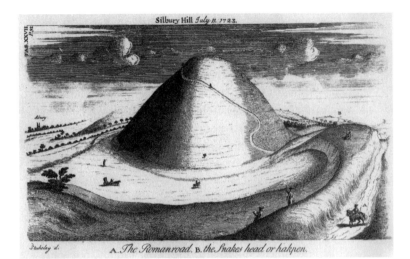

TAB. XXVII.
P. 82

Silbury Hill *July 11. 1723.*

Stukeley d.

A. *The Roman road.* B. *the Snakes head or hakpen.*

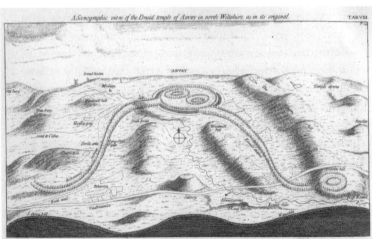

A Scenographic view of the Druid temple of ABVRY in north Wiltshire, as in its original.

TAB. VIII.
P. 32

ABVRY

Proehonorabili Dno. Dno. Philippo Dno. Hardwick, summo magnæ Britanniæ Cancellario tabulam. L.M.D. W. Stukeley.

W. Stukeley Delin.

hard-edged; he became obsessed with Stonehenge after a memorable moonlit visit as a student in 1921: 'I was alone and tremendously impressed.' Perhaps the lure was the way a standing stone seems poised between abstract monumentality and something softly figurative, ghostly, even human – shoulders, hollow of back, the curve of a hip. Did Moore ever depict Silbury? I think not, yet his lithographs of Stonehenge offer us a subjective, interior mystery that, if he had done so, might have taken our understanding of the hill in a startling direction.

Richard Long would clock the hill whenever he hitchhiked from his home in Bristol to London as a student: one of his earliest works, *A Line the Length of a Straight Walk from the Bottom to the Top of Silbury Hill*, was an installation piece in which he paced out the precise distance in a spiral of muddy footprints on a gallery carpet in New York's West Fifty-Seventh Street. It was created two years after Richard Atkinson's excavation was broadcast live on television in 1968. Straightness versus curve, masculine versus feminine. More recently the work has been re-installed as a neater, white-clay, slightly splashy spiral on various polished-wood gallery floors: Long, noting how 'powerful' the hill must once have been (finding its modern equivalent in the nuclear weapons research centre at Aldermaston), claims the piece is 'just another layer on the surface' shared by so many generations. He strongly objects, however, to his work being linked with prehistoric art, whose creations 'came about from a completely different culture … They were social, religious art. They were made by society. I make my work as an individual.'

Did he really go straight up? I've done so myself, stooped, pressing down on my thighs, panting, the grass rustling.

THE LEGEND OF SILBURY HILL

The townspeople of Marlborough and Devizes were always at loggerheads. Marlborough, coming off the worst at one fight, sought revenge by using the services of the Devil, who offered to wipe out Devizes by dropping a hill on the town. This threat was heard by St. John, who in due course warned Devizes. The townspeople of Devizes sent the biggest shoe, which had the Christ emblazoned, so put the Devil off... with a saint filled with old clothes and under his arm the Devil near Beckhampton, and there asked him the time... Old Nick was tired of carrying the hill, and asked in his turn how far to Devizes. The old man said that he should never get there that night or for some time to come, as he had left Devizes as a young man and had indeed worn out the clothes and shoes he was carrying – whereupon there on the patch he unloaded his hill. Old Nick was incredulous, but the old man stuck to his story, and dodged the Devil if so believing it... flung down the hill down from his shoulders the Devil departed in a flash of lightning. Devizes is still there. The hill at Silbury is for all to see. So the tale must be true.

The sculpture at this place
is the same length as a straight
walk from the bottom of Silbury
Hill in Wiltshire to the top.

First walked in North America, 1970.

Long's fresh layer is wafer-thin, like memory itself.

Silbury has gracefully posed for David Inshaw numerous times. His best-known depiction has her flickered about by lightning, the brilliant streaks reflected in the foreground waters of the Kennet stream: perhaps he sees nature as Gerard Manley Hopkins did, charged with creative energy (God, in the poet's case) – more inscape than landscape, with the Hill as a kind of battery.

He's finding, as Piper put it of his own work, 'something significant beyond ordinary significance'. Joe Tilson's origins were in Pop art, yet he effortlessly absorbed the deeper meanings of Wiltshire's chalklands when he moved there from London in 1970, with his trademark ziggurats chiming with the home-grown version that is Silbury. Writers such as Thomas Hardy and John Cowper Powys conjure a rather darker, animist power from downland sites like Stonehenge or Maiden Castle, rechannelling it through the inner lives of their characters: if our site was never part of their repertoire, something of that same drama and menace is felt in the composer Harrison Birtwistle's *Silbury Air*, written in direct response to the hill – which Birtwistle described oxymoronically as an 'artificial but organic intruder of the landscape'.

Intruder, yes. Organic *and* artificial.

Exactly.

Which brings us to the other Silbury-like native, Picked Hill. But despite appearances, it isn't artificial. Not surprisingly, it is a favoured place for some beautiful crop circle formations, and may well have been held in sacred esteem 5,000 years ago. Dr Jim Leary, the archaeologist who co-supervised Silbury's recent consolidation, suggests that it might be the latter's blueprint. Lying in the Vale of Pewsey south of Marlborough, the hill's abrupt shape is nevertheless shallower than Silbury's and not quite perfectly conical.

I would notice it forty years ago from the Kennet and Avon Canal that passes nearby: the Marlborough College Canal Society had just two boats and two members, me and a straggle-headed boy called Morrison, and we would mess about on Wednesday afternoons, entirely unsupervised. The wharf back then was a semi-abandoned spot facing a canal choked for much of its length by grass, waterweed and reeds between crumbling brick walls, with a huge abandoned barge still moored whose tarred wood would smell sweet when the sun warmed it. Our prow would probe into the floating sward and find discreet corridors. We mostly rowed, as the propellor kept having to be raised and freed of the canal's pungent tendrils: that way we could hear the plops of watervoles, wait for them to reappear. An otter. The iridescent blue fighter-plane swoop of a kingfisher. Everything lying further than the semi-clear stretches was mysterious, enticing, unattainable in a kind of verdant gloom. Something in me responds to dereliction, to ruins, in a regressive romanticism that is, I suppose, quite indefensible. Yet at one time this canal was high-tech, the very latest thing. Like Silbury, perhaps.

She is equally unattainable, but my internal prow can still probe her solitude, edging into the verdant gloom of her, of that great and derelict bulge. The angle of her slope is no sharper than a scarp, but scarps finish in a plateau that goes on and on. Scarp is edge, is tilt, is a kind of geological grinding along a fault-line. But Silbury's slope only flattens at the top for around 100 feet, with a discreet central hollow, then proceeds down again until it reaches ground. It is not quite symmetrically done – one flank (the southern) is shallower – but there is definite intent. You have the very peculiar sensation of something pushed up from underneath: a swelling, an eruption, perhaps a great laval bubble.

Or, less metaphorically, a barrow. A round barrow for King Sil, his likeness said to be mounted and in gold: a distant memory, claim some, of an excursion by Jesus in his missing years.

Silbury's size and steepness actually make her very different from a barrow. This is crucial. I would not be in love with Silbury if she was merely a Size XL barrow, a jumbo tumulus fit for a warrior legendary in his lifetime or for a king of egomaniacal tendencies. What's more, she was built in a flat-bottomed, moist valley, which is not what you do with a barrow.

The Danish for barrow means low. Although not as steep as in Stukeley's drawing of her, Silbury is not low. The government built some modern barrows recently, thirty of them, near Holsworthy: an entire grave complex not for humans but for dead cows during the BSE scare: hundreds of thousands of cows compressed into bin-liner smoulderings, floodlit, patrolled like an airbase, computer-monitored, a horrible smell. *The Times* called them 'Pharaonic tombs … the future will wonder at, as if some mysterious sacrifice has taken place.'

The future has already forgotten.

I lived up on the high downs for a while in the early 1980s, and would walk almost every day along a dry valley to the Four Barrows near Aldbourne, some ten miles from Silbury. My fondness for them led me, one pint-addled night, to face-paint myself with earth and lie on each of them in turn, star-shaped, spinning into the real constellations. The site was given added prestige by my discovering, with the help of a map and a ruler, that it lay directly on the major English ley line issuing from St Michael's Mount and running through Glastonbury to Bury St Edmund's Abbey and beyond, clipping various shrines dedicated to St Michael on the way Inevitable, given the number of the latter, say the doubters.

Perhaps this is why the very first paragraph of my very first work of fiction, *Ulverton*, features a barrow.

> He appeared on the hill at first light. The scarp was dark against a greening sky and there was the bump of a barrow and then the figure, and it shocked. I thought perhaps the warrior buried there had stood up again to haunt us. I thought this as I blew out the lanterns one by one around the pen. The sheep jostled and I was glad of their bells.

Way down below in the corner of the huge barley field lay a fifth and much larger tumulus – the famous Aldbourne barrow, covered in protective swirls of thick grass, again almost 100 feet across but no more than a man's height. From this shallow upturned bowl the tireless Victorians had trowelled out the compacted, chocolate-coloured fragments of what turned out to be a beautiful incense cup and its cover, along with the usual assortment of blades, awls, beads, rings, pebbles, boar tusks, arrowheads, sherds and flint flakes, plus a few burnt human bones covered in charcoal.

On the ridge to the west, in amongst a Mohican roach of beech trees, lurked the Giant's Grave, the biggest among a cemetery of five barrows, all likewise trowelled out in the ravenous nineteenth century. One early spring morning I stumbled across a shallow pit in there, half-hidden by branches and fallen leaves: lying in the pit was a cartload of sheep skulls, like the aftermath of a catastrophe. The winter had been very severe – a few people had actually died of exposure up on the downs, where the winds were razor-sharp and there was no shelter: one man had frozen to death in his car. Were these the result? Surely not: flesh takes longer to drop off, and these bones were clean. A farmer's cull? A serious outbreak of foot rot or scrapie? Was this type of mass burial even legal? The barrow loomed in the distance through the smooth-trunked trees, the dead leaves rustled in the wind like my endless suppositions. I imagined being watched by the farmer, cradling a shotgun and marking me down as a meddling incomer – or worse: as a danger that had to be dealt with.

Rustling suppositions, stories unravelling. Imagination thrives on mystery. The puritan landowners and farmers who, out of genuine belief or straightforward greed or a canny mixture of both, brought down most of the standing stones and flattened numerous tumuli in the area's immediate ritual landscape, liked neither mystery nor the fructifying imagination. It is depressing that this extraordinary landscape, whose minimum area of nine square miles includes Avebury henge, the Sanctuary, the two great Avenues, East and West Kennet Long Barrow, Windmill Hill, the Marlborough Mound and various barrow cemeteries, and for which Silbury may have been the symbolic centre, had not exerted a more positive pull on their vision of life. But if, Taliban-like, they believed, as did their medieval forerunners, that the stones and barrows were the Devil's work, this was not the result of imagination so much as logic: these bizarre elements in the landscape were not Christian, *ergo* they were heathen.

Avebury and Stonehenge are built mostly in sarsen stone, this being a type of sandstone harder than granite, its great scattered boulders left like rubble after glaciation had smashed the sandstone cap that covered most of southern England some three million years ago. The boulders are the mere core, in turn, of much larger blocks that have been weathered away to their present shape. The absolute neutrality of geology was yet to impinge on these pre-Darwinian farmers:

'sarsen' is a corruption of 'saracen'. The destruction of these temples was therefore a type of crusade. The fact that they feared the stones and barrows might suggest some sort of imaginative tendency, but of the flickery type that feeds on credulousness and anxiety and is easily fanned by those who like to manipulate others for their own ends: men like John Baker and his successor John Bale, nonconformist preachers at Avebury, fulminating against idolatry from their sarsen-built and well-thronged Meeting House.

When the so-called Sanctuary, a magnificent stone circle on Overton Hill, was ripped out by the terrible Farmer Green in 1724, the other locals were very upset. Maybe there were quite a few among them who practised pagan ways, homeopathic magic, whether or not they were churchgoing. Or maybe their internal landscape was wedded to the outer, their memories so bound up with the earth and place that to see this great ripple of stones removed in a matter of days hurt them psychically in some way. But Green owned land and was part of a matrix of local power that was unassailable.

I see labouring men and women lining the entrance to the Sanctuary, spreading out their ranks along the sunken and rutted breadth of the Bath Road up there on the hill, now a dangerously blind exit from the Ridgeway car park. Green clops up on his horse, scattering flints from the hooves: he is a plump, red-faced, Hogarthian figure in a tricorn hat and double-breasted coat with flapped pockets, his thick neck hidden under a knotted cravat. He might not have been plump, of course: he might have been cavernously thin, consumed by covetousness and a puritan zeal.

It was Stukeley, without whose painstaking records we would know much less about the Avebury complex, who recorded the general sorrow in the work that brought the area immediate fame: *Abury, a Temple of the British Druids, with Some Others Described* (1743):

> This *Overton-Hill*, from time immemorial, the country people have a high notion of. It was (alas, it was!) a very few years ago, crown'd with a most beautiful temple of the Druids. They still call it the sanctuary ...the loss of this work I did not lament alone; but all the neighbours (except the person that gain'd the little dirty profit) were heartily griev'd for it. It had a beauty that touch'd them far beyond those much greater circles in Abury town.

I see the pitchforks shake and rise a little as Green and his henchmen approach like the bad guys in a Western. His eyes flicker to the circle of sarsens in that tilth, that fertile acreage of which he has already calculated the profit, not dirty at all to him. But something else drives him: he is addicted to pulling out the stones, the rotten teeth of the land, to reducing the devilish ache of the land. He has extracted and smashed so many already, down there in the village, that he feels lighter in his head, he sleeps more easily despite his poor digestion, his tendency to wind. He smells of sweat, manure and the cologne his wife brought from her London trip, returning with an absurd coiffure that brushed against the low beams. She fancies his work is dangerous: that it meddles with the Devil, and that a stone might crush him (or a part of him) flat. His work does have his dangers, which is why he is addicted. He has brought along his usual hip flask of rum: Dutch courage. Anyway, it is bitter cold up here. But like so many individuals with or without psychopathic leanings, he justifies his destruction by saying it is God's work, just as slave owners whip their slaves because the Bible says you can. He even believes it himself.

And now he is confronted by the Devil's minions, a mob from all around, among whom he recognises certain faces. Instantly a bile of rage rises in his mouth and he tastes future vengeances, petty or otherwise. Green is a nasty man. His type of nastiness has peppered history from unrecorded times. Up to now, he has never been stopped, because his type are almost impossible to stop. His energy, focussed down on one narrow point, is inexhaustible.

They say he has plans to flatten Silbury Hill, visible from here as a mere wart to the west. In truth, this is more a fantasy than a plan. He dreams of it at night when he lies awake beside his snoring wife. But he has no idea how to go about it. It is too big for the plough blade, of course, too steep for the horses: it would need several lifetimes, unless an army could be yoked to the task. He visualises hundreds of men made miniature by the enormity of the devilish boil, wielding spades for days, weeks, months, even years, lancing the swelling in a complex operation that would be known of throughout the kingdom. King George would visit, marvelling at what can be done in God's name.

And Green imagines the hill years later as a gentle, spade-gouged hummock, his own face swept by a white beard, and then sees his own ploughs striping a flat, somewhat claggy field where once the Devil had exposed his stinking buttocks. He might even hold a picnic there in celebration, attended by local dignitaries and powerful friends, the type that are invited to those piss-ups in the grounds of what was the old Seymour house in Marlborough. '*Fêtes galantes*', they call them. He'll give them a Frenchie feast, alright. And then he might die, at peace with his conscience and a life's task fulfilled.

This is the man confronting the rabble. But though he might shout, he is powerless to break through their ranks: when the mob start to throw stones, his henchmen flee. He is pulled off his horse and cuffed and kicked, barely escaping with his life. The beautiful ripple of stones is saved from its sleep of some 4,000 years or more and remains intact to our day – Farmer Green never returning, dying of apoplexy soon after.

Alas, this is a counter-factual fantasy. The stone circle known as the Sanctuary is now a misery of concrete markers: when excavated in the 1930s by Maud Cunnington (a novelist could not have invented that name), the stoneholes had very little in them besides the shards of broken sarsen left by our hero. Nobody took action in 1724, cowed as they were by the local power patterns and by the general fashion for destruction – its fierce self-righteousness having a bit more edge than the status quo of leaving well alone, leaving things as they had always been, letting the grass grow long around the stony feet where the sheep nibble in the shadow out of the wind, century after century.

Unlike Silbury, the four Aldbourne humps and most of the hundreds of others on the downland have yielded urns and bones and ashes, given up their crouched dead. They are tombs for individuals, not a huddled collective like the long barrows: private rooms, not dormitories. Around 2500 BC, this individualism begins to leave its trace on the landscape; attributed to the arrival of the Beaker culture from the Continent, it comes with cord-patterned drinking vessels (like beakers), metal-working (copper and then bronze), alcohol (a potent honey mead), barley crops, weaving and some sophisticated archery equipment. No one can establish whether this shift came on the bloody edge of a copper blade, through the pacific allure of trade goods or via a steady trickle of big-boned, stylish newcomers. Archaeologists are deeply divided on the issue. It is far less clear than the equivalent if equally complex shift we call the Italian Renaissance in the literate fifteenth century.

If, as some believe, Silbury was actually built, or at least inspired, by these Beaker folk, might they have been bringing along some vision of home? Except that no one has agreed where home was for these continentals, or if there was a home as such. Their pottery and individual graves are scattered all over Europe. They seem to have been highly mobile go-getters, tall and famously square-headed – impressive-looking, in other words, and so well able to boss the indigenes about with the help of a miraculous metal flashing from their weapons.

Furthermore, as far as Silbury is concerned, recent excavations have proved that the extraordinary final vision was not even there at the beginning: the site yields a long series of developments, of stops and starts, between around 2400 BC and 2300 BC. From a little cairn of gravel (perhaps marking or 'sealing' a sacred or ceremonial place), she rose to the great white mound at the end of an effort that lasted three or four generations and involved several rather piecemeal phases. 'Build me a mountain!' does not seem to have been a big-boned order, whether Beaker or native. And if these new arrivals preferred their elite to be tucked up inside an individual mound, then Silbury's emptiness does not fit at all.

Unless, of course, a great tombless mound is a kind of

cultural hybrid: migrating cultures have a habit of assimilating local influences. Perhaps Silbury's strangeness may just be the result of an intermingling, the creation of a new, third space that had no antecedents and, in terms of sheer scale at least, no offspring: an overlapping of periods – the late Neolithic and the early Bronze Age – which constitutes a unique cultural moment.

Indeed, so complex are the prehistoric migration patterns of our continent that the whole Beaker question remains a problem: until recently archaeologists preferred a simple shuttling to and fro of cultural influence, a progression (and often regression or even loss) of technical knowledge which wove new patterns without the help of a colourful cast of lofty immigrants emerging up the beach or out of the woods. These days, however, we prefer to see domination as a key factor. Coercion, even. But uncertainty prevails: some experts posit a wave of sophisticated peoples from the east (possibly West Asia), others that the shift spread north and east from a Beaker cluster in Iberia.

The times project their own preferences onto the far and unworded past.

The presence of Beaker vessels in burials by the Avebury stones stir, as ever, more questions than answers: it might just point to a certain taste in pottery; or the sacrifice of a convenient stranger; or a foreign elite directly responsible for building these mammoth new works – for expanding them, at least. The recently discovered grave of the so-called Amesbury Archer near Stonehenge, dating from around the time the great stones were being dragged in and erected (towards the end of Silbury's construction) – suggests the latter. He was brought up in the Alps and was probably a coppersmith as well as an archer; he suffered chronic pain from an abscess and a missing kneecap that had left his bone infected. The richness of the grave goods (they included three copper knives and several gold ornaments) indicate that he was someone who mattered, albeit with a bad limp and no doubt grumpy from his ills. Just being a coppersmith would have given him the status of a mage: the ability not to adapt a material but to transmute it into something else. As a god does.

It doesn't take much for a powerful, innovative culture to spread through simple osmosis: look at the US, from Hollywood to hamburgers. The Beaker shift might also have been helped by a new idea: kingship, or at least chieftainship. Other barrows close to Stonehenge have similarly yielded gold-peppered graves that suggest an elite: as with city real estate near a tube station, the hot property in tombs was measured in distance from the place that mattered. Individualism, again. Recent analyses even suggest that the initial arrival of a few was not followed by the many, and that health may have played a part: Beaker skeletons indicate their owners were on better physical form than the locals – or at least those from the early Neolithic (there isn't much in the way of bones from the later Neolithic).

Apart from this confusion, those hundreds of round tumuli are not a mystery, not an enigma. Barrows are known throughout the world as a form of grave without the gravestone, a visible honouring or recollection of the departed, somewhere in which he or she might sleep the long sleep. The rituals change from place to place, era to era, but most involve depositing goods – personal ornaments or tools – to accompany the dead person on his long journey in the afterlife. Flower petals have been found in a Neanderthal grave, probably cast in as the simplest form of metaphoric or symbolical reflection. The human rituals and thoughtscapes of prehistory – a period which takes up all but the last few millennia's tiny fraction of our total time on Earth so far – remain closed to us, since history begins with writing and only writing records such things. There are still preliterate peoples surviving today, much closer than we are to the Neolithic in their lifestyles, but extrapolating the deep past from their living present can only ever be another type of informed guesswork.

All we do know from their example is what unimaginable effort it takes to build great mounds and stone circles and chambered tombs.

Literacy doesn't cover everything – far from it. I have no idea what Farmer Green was really like, I have made an informed guess which is part-projection tinted with my own anger and grief, but knowing the complexities of human nature (Wiltshire farmers included), his real self may well have surprised me by its pot-house jollity, its rollicking charm – think of Stalin's avuncular mask, or Mao's friendly grin. Unlikely, given Stukeley's report ('dirty little profit' sounds like an echo of local anger, Wiltshire-burred), but there is simply no means of knowing.

Similarly, we can map deep into the universe, we can reconstruct its origins down to the last millisecond – all but look into the eye of God, as it were – by listening to the echoes of the Big Bang still rippling out after billions of years, but the single thud of a ritual drum high up on Silbury has vanished for ever and can never be restored.

Three

So Silbury is empty, as far as we are concerned. Empty of our usual expectations. Empty of what might illuminate. Materially, of course, she is far from empty. She is filled in above her lower ditch-surrounded section of white bedrock by hundreds of tons of chalk and sarsen. But the hill is, intellectually, a mystery that flirts with the void. Symmetrical and lovely, visually powerful, visible for miles around, dramatic even under grass, she is almost sullen in her unyieldingness.

My physics teacher at Marlborough, Frank McKim – the only person who has ever brought that subject to life for me, so that I was near top of the class for a year instead of near bottom – probed that void by conducting a resistivity survey in 1959. A buried tomb would show up as a significant oscillation, offering more resistance to the current carried between the steel probes. I have seen, either in a book I can't find or in a dream, a photograph of Marlborough College boys in their grey jackets and blue ties clustered around the instrument's dial or helping their teacher (a 'beak' in college argot) unwind the cable and set the probes.

The needle trembled only faintly as the probe sensed different resistances in the dumped chalk. Then all of a sudden, as in the best adventure films, it wavered wildly and leapt up, quivering. There was a swell of excitement among the boys in their close-shorn fifties haircuts, already thrilled to be out of the glorified prison camp with its cold baths and dormitory fumblings, its secret terrorisings, the gloomy classrooms of North Block, and into this immense earth-smelling airy openness a few miles up the road – where, for all the white-coated scientific underpinning (as trusty and sensible as a nuclear power plant) they were hunting for treasure. There were shrieks, cries of 'Golly, look at that, sir!' in old BBC-announcer voices that mimicked their professional, pipe-puffing fathers. Frank McKim smiled and nodded, his enthusiasm always gentle: but his eyes glittered with excitement. Did he know from the start that this blip was not the anomaly of a vault full of riches fit for King Sil, but the iron-bound door placed there by Dean John Merewether of the Royal Archaeological Institute to block access to the tunnel he excavated in 1849? I have no idea, as I wasn't there and I don't know any ex-pupil who was.

Except for the man himself. I did ask him about this treasure hunt once, after a lesson: a complete non-scientist who loathed the stink of the labs, I was willing to sacrifice my sticky-buns tea just to chat to him now and again. He chuckled, and admitted he had been disappointed. 'It's probably just one big lump of chalk,' he said, holding up the stubby example that had done service during the lesson. 'A mystery.'

A few years before this, Professor Richard Atkinson had followed McKim with a massive series of excavations and analyses that made Silbury a temporary TV celebrity: the operation was followed live by *Chronicle*, presented by Magnus

Magnusson. Although my selective memory has occluded the black-and-white excitement of it, I do remember the eventual disappointment. Deducting from other great mounds in the world, Atkinson reckoned that Silbury was a giant tomb, and went in primarily via the 1849 tunnel left by Merewether. The hill was pocked, prodded, drilled into and 'X-rayed' with a seismograph; the results were revealing in terms of the nitty-gritty of construction, but televisually undramatic (despite tunnel roof collapses): there was no buried gold or royal skeleton. Silbury is no Sutton Hoo.

However, my wife's brother recalls being driven up the Bath Road from Wimbledon by my mother-in-law in the summer of 1968 to view the hill in the flesh, so excited was she by the programme. 'This was not her usual mode,' he added: Silbury had exerted a pull.

Despite this precedent, I was crestfallen by that metonymic stub of chalk: I'd hoped for a crazed gleam in my teacher's eye, a glimpse of secret knowledge, something only he had felt during the experiment or had noticed the needle do. Next to me was the class boffin, a bespectacled boy with twig-like limbs whose vicar father was a well-known if controversial exorcist. I regarded this boy, who suffered teasing and bullying with an almost menacing equanimity, as the local expert in all things occult. If I saw a ghost – which I did several times during my school sojourn – he was the first port of call. He would treat the event in the way a birdwatcher treats the sighting of an unusual bird: he converted the spirit world into the normalcy of the scientific.

My problem, *pace* Frank McKim, was that I found the scientific world abnormal. I hated the white concrete cuboids of the Science Labs and most particularly their interior smell, a hellish potpourri of formaldehyde, leaking gas from bunsen burners and the gigantic flatulence of hydrogen sulphide. It gave me a headache; these days it would be shut down until the proper systems were installed, but forty years ago such a chemical fug equalled Science in Action, so was good in the way blood streaked on faces in a game of rugger was good.

There was a tank full of huge locusts whose pointless existence seemed typified in the fact that they appeared to be eating each other with relish, crawling over severed limbs and carcasses with clockwork abandon. The existential despair this provoked was heightened by a crude fresco of dinosaurs covering the upper half of an entire wall, a fearsome *Tyrannosaurus rex* summing up the whole enterprise: Nature has no morals, we are all the chance product of a glorified chemical soup, and the predatory college world is essentially a jungle with zits – a faithful reflection of the universe, then, but on a minuscule scale somewhere in Wiltshire.

It was a shock, beginning my boarding school career at

thirteen. And I had been a reasonably happy schoolboy up to then, taking the Green Line bus or being dropped off by my father at the school gates on his way to work at Heathrow.

His work was soon to take him abroad again – Kabul was mooted, or Kathmandu, or Kinshasa. Before we moved to Chesham in 1962, my early life had been peripatetic. I stare out nonplussed from the little square Rolleiflex snaps, with various exotic locations as a backdrop – either because these constituted home, or we were visiting via a free flight in a Pan Am quad-prop: Paris (where I was born), Lebanon (where we were briefly ambushed in the mountains near Beirut during the '58 uprising), Calcutta (where my mother nearly died of dysentery), Kathmandu (long before the hippies arrived), Bangkok (where we pose in an empty temple courtyard) and so on. I don't suppose I had a clue how lucky I was, or even what 'exotic' meant. Standing in blazing sun by some ancient masterwork in the smells of Asia or the Middle East before mass tourism had even been thought of…this was normal to me. But what effect did it have on my consciousness? Certainly not a desire to be a world traveller.

Maybe my obsession with Silbury Hill is another kind of subliminal rooting. After Calcutta, my father was posted to Heathrow. My first memory of England is walking through a huge field of grass with my brother (eight years older than me) behind our temporary rented home in Chertsey. Because I was only four and a half, the grass seemed immensely high, spattered with brilliant spots of sunlight. Maybe Chertsey was less suburban then. Maybe I thought all England was like this.

One reason my father opted for the foreign postings was because it meant Pan Am paid for his children's schooling… for the privilege of a public school education. My father knew nothing about public schools; my grandfather had been his headmaster, first at the village school and then at Matlock Bank's C of E. My mother had been an evacuee in the war and had loved it.

Within moments of waving them goodbye on Marlborough College's sweeping gravel drive, a leg shot out in front of me as I entered my junior house and I was sent sprawling. 'I'm Hawks-Gibbet,' said the leg's owner, 'and don't you forget it.' I did, because he was eminently forgettable ('Hawks-Gibbet' is invented, of course). Others weren't. Most had been boarding since the age of seven, or earlier. They knew the codes, and had grown inured to a lack of affection. They had, in a way, gone tribal – without the blood-kinship of a true tribe.

My junior house was designed by a Victorian builder of prisons, Edward Blore. It was three floors high, a lumpen cube

of brooding red brick with a deep central well descending vertiginously to the basement; this void was skirted round on each floor by railed-off galleries, with dormitories instead of cells. Everything echoed. I was deep in the skirts of the Victorian period, including a smell of boiled beef and drains.

There was something else. Our initiation ceremony would apparently involve crossing the void hand over hand on a knotted rope of bed sheets. Back in the late nineteenth century, a knot had come undone and a new boy had plunged to his death and now haunted the basement as a pale apparition. He had left a faint discolouration on the basement's stone floor like the bare chalk on Dragon Hill.

Looking up at the third-floor level high above, I wondered whether he had had time to scream, whether he had known what was happening in those few seconds of fall. These questions were especially riveting when you were on lock-up duty, alone in the basement at night, switching off the lights one by one behind you, your torch wavering over the discolouration. He'd been seen standing there, or his scream had been heard. During that first term, the thought of having to cross that soaring shadowy space for myself hand over hand added another coat of anxiety to the glutinous impasto of my general state. ('It's definitely planned for tomorrow night,' a particularly eager boy in our dorm regularly reassured us from out of the darkness.) The relief when I learned from a gentle giant in the year above that we had – ho ho – been 'had', felt like the lifting of a death sentence: maybe the whole tragic account was itself just a sadistic myth.

Years later, I learned that it wasn't. During my gap year, my parents had come back from Africa to a hamlet at the foot of the Berkshire downs. A neighbour turned out to be an Old Marlburian, and at some point during a village gathering he told me that his father had been holding one end of the sheet when 'that poor boy fell to his death in 'A' House. What? Oh yes, he made an awful racket as he went. The worst, though, was when he hit.'

Legend was suddenly converted into concrete fact: what had seemed misty and far off now felt too close: I was holding onto a rope of knotted sheets called time, and could feel the tremors and twitches of the past. It was a kind of recovered memory.

The dorm where I spent my first night as a boarder looked directly out on a steep, overgrown slope full of trees and bushes. This was one side of Merlin's Mound, or simply 'the Mound', another (if smaller) artificial hill: Merlin was

buried in it, thus the name. It, too, was haunted – by the wizard himself. But that was not the reason it was strictly forbidden to climb it: theoretically, it was an ancient monument, though a much-neglected one, with a Victorian water tank occupying the top and a crumbling eighteenth-century grotto in its flank doubling as a bike-shed. I was startled, looking out of the window into the blackness, to hear voices from the steep foliage, to see red pinprick eyes winking and blinking, until a sharp whiff of tobacco explained it.

My bed consisted of an old black-iron frame, springs that had long lost their spring and a horse-hair mattress that had moulded itself to the dip in the middle, which was faintly stained. There was a label stitched onto the mattress with '1909' printed on it in faded black, and the springs screeched every time I moved. The Great War poet Charles Hamilton Sorley, killed during the Battle of Loos in 1915 at the age of twenty, had endured exactly the same sack, judging from a photograph in his biography. Next to each bed was a narrow wooden locker that kept the beds from touching. There were at least twenty beds in the high-ceilinged room. There was

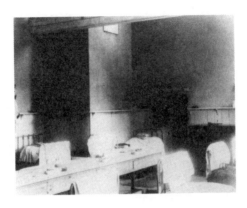

a complete lack of privacy, something John Betjeman had found equally challenging about Marlborough around half a century earlier, the Chapel being the 'only place where I could be alone'. Apart from the dizzying spaces of the 'golden downs', of course.

Your locker in the dorm and, in the 'prep' room, your small desk-and-shelf unit known as a 'horsebox', were islands of fragile selfhood and very rarely invaded. This seems surprising, now I think about it, given the atavistic pressures, the general brutishness: my previous experience of boarders had been through total immersion in the Jennings books by Anthony Buckeridge, but the only similarity to his characters' geniality was the exclusive use of surnames. *Tom Brown's Schooldays* was closer to the reality, even in its analysis of how weak 'no-government' is worse than a 'rough' but 'just' rule. In 1970, Marlborough was setting the pace for the liberal type of public school, stressing the arts, introducing girls in the sixth form, permitting longish hair (a terrible mistake in stylistic terms – it might have worked more or less on Black Sabbath or Deep Purple, but not on adolescents sinking under acne). The loosening effect at the lower form level was well-meaning but ultimately proved Thomas Hughes's observation: 'boys follow one another in herds like sheep, for good or evil; they hate thinking, and have rarely any settled principles.'

When we had to read *Lord of the Flies* by William Golding, I found it eerily familiar. Golding was brought up in Marlborough, and attended the grammar school, where his father taught science, but it was Bishop Wordsworth's School in Salisbury – where he taught for a while – that inspired the novel. When I became a full-time writer, Golding was already my master: his novel *The Inheritors*, taking us into the Neanderthal mind, is an underrated masterpiece of twentieth-century literature. It is undoubtedly influenced by Wiltshire and its 'particularly ancient and mysterious history that has left its mark in every corner,' as Golding rather dutifully put it, adding 'almost every question we ask about that history goes unanswered, and tantalizes.' He was peculiarly sensitive to that history: his beautiful old family house on the green backed onto the churchyard and gave him bad dreams for the rest of his life. Yet he stayed in the county, because it was home, and because of 'the austere beauty of [its] ancient face.'

He hated the College, like many in the town, because he resented its privilege. The swagger and bray of some of its pupils still force locals off the pavement: this happened to me a few years ago, returning to see our friends Sasha and Ray Ward, whose children went to Golding's school. I was once one of these, I thought. The College seams the town with money and jobs, emanates a certain cultural and intellectual forcefield, but has become even more absurdly privileged (a year's fees equal a decent salary), and now boasts a princess, the wife of both the present prime minister and his chancellor, and the future king's spouse as Old Marlburiennes, as well as the homesick progeny of Russian billionaires.

I have never met anyone who was happy at school in their early teens, whether day or boarding, state or private: an excruciating period of pimply transition is simply rendered worse by the very form of most education systems – liberal or disciplinarian, it makes little difference. But for those pupils with what might be called manipulative personality disorder, boarding school is an open field 24/7, and liberal-minded Marlborough College in the 1970s was peculiarly open. One sixth-form boy in the grim senior house I went up to in my second year – let's call him Philip – had lost his father in an air crash: his greasy, elbow-length hair and a tendency to sadistic manipulation were genially tolerated. He was, in fact, given carte blanche. Although I had firmly refused his sexual advances, I had to perform two tasks that some might see as substitution (or, if not, then for some deeper maternal or paternal lack): washing his hair and telling him bedtime stories.

Every three weeks or so he would lie back in one of the cast-iron, claw-footed bathtubs lined up in our common bathroom with its long row of basins, its communal showers and loos without locks, and I would knead his pulpy, slippery, Lynyrd Skynyrd mane. Every three days or so I had to entertain him (and the entire dorm) after lights out with improvised stories, delivered while sitting on the edge of his bed like… well, a father. This last therapeutic service would have been fine except that if he wasn't sufficiently entertained, I was punished in various ways familiar to professional torturers.

Unfortunately, the technique used by Scheherazade to save her life – stopping in the middle of a story as dawn broke – was not workable, as I would rarely go on beyond midnight. By keeping to ghosts, humour and general suspense, I mostly jammed my way out of punishment, even earning a certain sobriquet as a yarn-spinner. When he was satisfied – once acknowledging, at the end of a particularly complex concoction, 'That was really good'– I would feel a warm flush of pride.

This exercise might, I suppose, have helped me in my future career as a fiction writer, the consequences when I failed being a physical counterpart to a bad review: his thumb and forefinger once held my right nipple in a vice for at least two minutes, leaving a livid aureole that lasted most of the term. I can still see his face as he squeezed, his eyes seeking mine with a gleeful determination full, I suppose, of rage against the fate that had snatched his dad. I would almost have preferred to have been roasted against an open fire like Tom Brown, a character I very much saw as my predecessor.

Philip was nearly as bad as my chief tormentor, a black-haired, squat boy of inordinate strength, malignity and wealth, whose sister had died of a drug overdose. He delighted in calling me 'Mr Average' and would sidle up with a stage-villain cackle in class and prophesy various unpleasant things that were to happen to me that night. Mostly he would descend to simple brutishness – one favourite was to hurl metal-studded boots as I shielded myself behind rugby kit in the changing-room. My academic prowess being understandably damaged under this treatment, he overtook me and left a year earlier, to my great relief.

I could dig a tunnel into this darkness, this great mound

of oblivion, the blind marl of the unsaid heaped up and now grassed over after decades, and reveal deeper horrors that I have learned about since. But why disturb?

No digging. Climbing forbidden.

My only physical means of escape was, of course, to venture into the immediate countryside. At first I found the chalk downland forbiddingly bleak, far less cosy than the chalk hills I was used to – the beech-wooded, kindly Chilterns in home-counties Bucks.

But I was, in one sense, jump-started.

A week into term we were all forced to go on a sponsored walk, the start of a school tradition that now involves twenty miles of cheery stuff along the prehistoric Ridgeway's glutinous track in funny hats and costumes, and forty-three years ago was a serious-minded thirty-mile slog. In 1970 it wandered across some of the most impressive of Wiltshire's crests and scarps and combes, not only tramping the Ridgeway – I recall being impressed by Hackpen Hill – but also tackling the claggiest of enormous fields. I saw what I thought was a flock of sheep, but they were recumbent sarsens, so we must have gone by the dry, thistled valley of Fyfield Down or perhaps through the thatched village of Lockeridge, its cottages contemplating a grassy field that swirls between the sarsens like a flood.

Within half an hour of setting out, the gallant eight hundred had thinned into a sparse and unsupervised straggle, and I was being dragged towards an electric fence, assured that the shock would kill me. I soon settled into the rhythm of the slow miles, careful to keep my mouth mostly shut, judging which informal group of walkers held out the promise of civility rather than savagery, and almost enjoying myself. I had no idea where I was at any point, as cartographic knowledge belonged to a higher order of being whose voices were broken, as did everything else. Homesick, psychologically as well as literally bruised after a week of my new existence (I had already been thrashed by my housemaster), I felt a vague enmity towards the landscape, not helped by said housemaster's choice of after-prep reading: Bunyan's *The Pilgrim's Progress*. The Wiltshire downs were tinged with the grimness of the dorms, the collective Victorian bathrooms, the pack mentality of the incumbents, the sunless classrooms in North Block, and not being in the hills around Chesham. I began to feel really tired and peckish at about seventeen miles.

There was uncertainty as to the route, and I followed those who were making their way across a flint-strewn field, singing, my army corps boots adding several pounds to their weight in the form of white-streaked tilth. The last ten miles saw many faltering and dropping out, and I imagined them being summarily shot for desertion. Meanwhile I was in an advanced state of hunger, the odd quarter of orange at the infrequent check-points merely adding to the pain. We were promised a slap-up meal with the Master if we completed the full thirty miles.

At one late point, in the middle of a fervent imagining of our favourite foods – I think it must have been along a rutted stretch of the Ridgeway – we passed under a long avenue of trees and I had what I was eventually to call, in my brief Zen period, a 'satori' moment. A high without drugs, a spikenard fume of bliss in your head, a glimpse of some universal heaven, but intimately connected with the sensual reality around you. The scent of resin from a sun-warmed pine tree had always done this for me, and still does.

My introduction to the downs was complete.

When I got to the finishing tape, almost dead and avid for my slap-up meal, I was asked brusquely if I had taken the 'short cut' across that claggy field. My hesitant answers meant that I had to walk a further two miles around and around the orange futility of the running track in a gathering darkness, alone apart from the pedant of a teacher in his tracksuit, notebook poised.

I knew waiting for school's boarding by the bingo hall in Watford
the coach would come, the inevitability of deathly things,

sad things, the sadness in me always like a thorn, coach-sick –
then staring at my reflection in the coach's glass

as it trembled up the broad road past homes and windows
to the black Wiltshire spaces, downs, like space itself

a vacuum into which I am thrown, the pure unknown,
reluctant, sickly with fear, bullies' thrones on knees before,

sick for home or for my own career, not bred for this,
England-outsider, not quite stranger but not friend either, nor
foe.

It was my bicycle – or 'grid' in the curious school argot – that took me deepest into the landscape's open airiness. I was used to beechwoods in the Chilterns, where they spread for miles, their columnar spaciousness like multiple cathedral interiors, their leaves like stained glass allowing a flood of greenish-gold light to penetrate on sunlit days. On the downs, however, they mostly existed as clumps, copses where you could see the edges from the middle. Vast and ancient

Savernake Forest, spreading south-east of Marlborough just a short walk from the College gates, was full of thick-boled oaks and felt dark and primordial to a schoolboy seeking air and light, though I would venture there occasionally with a friend.

I have a vivid memory of sitting in a spinney up on the downs among electric-blue sheets of bluebells on a day of sun, blissfully alone, just where the smooth trunks of the beeches petered out into a grassy expanse, munching on the snack I'd bought in my pannier and thinking I was in heaven. If only life could be this, this alone, and not the other. School existed as a lumpy, granular mess somewhere out there (really, just a few miles away), like a labyrinthine heap of rubble the size of a city, incomprehensible, stalked by fiends, with the odd sun-shaft of poetry both literal and metaphorical.

Heaven, hell.

But my ticking wheels, and sometimes my legs alone (although these could never do me the same miles or give me that freewheeling rush), were my secret passage out, the Colditz tunnel to somewhere no one could touch me.

I never went very far: the times when you were liberated from lessons, games, corps, meals, Chapel or various 'creative' activities were almost non-existent in the week, which left Wednesday and Saturday and Sunday afternoons. But I went far enough to feel, in my early teens, a kind of *Shropshire Lad* solitariness, a roaming freedom. I was constructing something separate and independent through a love of landscape, animals, trees and clean skies that was forming, I suppose, my adult personality. One sunny day in May our young art teacher took us out *plein air* painting on a stretch of the River Kennet by the school water meadows: I found

ows or in the extraordinary lost world
shallow scrubland valley from where
l out for the great rings, and where
lithic axes on a polishing stone? Or
s like ghosts or shadows or invisible

myself disappearing into the complexity of the vegetation, its highlights and shadows and myriad greens and browns, my brush helplessly swirling the gouache until time itself seemed suspended. Oddly, my memory of that double lesson remains vivid and precise. Something had coursed through me and lifted me out of gloom.

I joined the Natural History Society, but our trips out to various nature spots were marred by the nausea produced by a stuffy car. We never walked the downs, oddly: the complex mat of the grazed grass hid flowers (harebell, wild thyme, milkwort, orchids, bird's foot trefoil) whose names I was determined to learn; my Derbyshire father and grandmother knew all the wild flowers, as if they had imbibed their names at birth – albeit northern monikers. I was a hopeless bird-spotter, too. What turned me on far more than the flickery silhouette of a bunting or a shrike was a general feeling of well-being: lofty tree-crowns blurred and waving in fresh gusts; the edge of a meadow darkened into mystery by a straggly blackthorn hedge; the intimacy of a single cornflower that no one else would ever notice; the scuffles of secret little beasts through dead leaves or grass, untainted by the absurdity of human institutions. Half a night spent up a tree near the same school water meadows fruitlessly watching for badgers, my companion on the branch (the son of the exorcist) moaning from fear of falling off, spelt the end of my Society outings.

And then there was the prehistoric. Tumuli lumped on the crests or crouched in the woods. The tunnel darkness of the long barrows. The enigmatic humanoid suggestion of the upright sarsens, whereas the prone monoliths were always startlingly sheep-like, thus their local name: Grey Wethers.

This all slightly frightened me, at least in the first two years. Louis MacNeice, another Marlburian, seems to have felt the same way:

> ...here in the first
>
> Inhabited heights of chalk I could feel my mind
> Crumble and dry like a fossil sponge, I could feel
> My body curl like a foetus and the rind
>
> Of a barrow harden round me, to reveal
> Millennia hence some inkling of the ways
> Of man before he invented plough or wheel
>
> Or before England, still in her foetal daze
> Of forest and fen, had cut the umbilical cord
> That bound her to the Continent. It pays,
>
> In adolescence, not to face that horde
> Of Stone Age men...

He has it exactly, despite his chronological muddling. Your psyche is altered by this area, he says. This is because, as a teenager, you are relatively new to existence. Attending boarding school for five years in the middle of what was our island's greatest sacred land temple affects the process of assimilating the mystery of why you are here at all. As he drives past the school gates on the Bath Road in the 1950s, MacNeice relives

> ...the thoughts, the shadows, that used to walk
> Beside me on these downs that carve the sky
> With a clean indifferent sweep...

That mention of 'shadows' interests me: why does he equate thoughts with shadows, or does he mean that indefinable presence, that haunting sense you feel on the

Ridgeway or by th
of Fyfield Down,
the sarsens were
you find marks of
are thoughts them
companions?

A housemaster once showed me MacNeice's signature in a leather-bound house rota from 1922, recording various duties fulfilled: it was small and cowering and trembly: *F.L. MacNeice*. He found the school cruel, as I did, in his junior years – but flowered, as I did, in the last two, similarly nurturing his poetry. Beyond was the indifference of those sweeping spaces and the lost echoes of the prehistoric hordes.

I am perhaps exaggerating my solitariness, especially as the terms passed. There were deeply sympathetic and inspiring teachers who opened myriad doors, especially to literature and theatre and history and art, and who encouraged our green shoots of learning with a master-gardener's patience and respect. Good friends were also made who are still close to my heart four decades later.

One wintry Sunday when I was about fifteen, three of us went off on our 'grids' to treasure hunt in East Kennet Long Barrow, the neglected sibling of the celebrated West Kennet version. Stranded in a field, East Kennet had no public access and was unexcavated; more mystery, forbidden territory – the essential ingredients for boyish adventure. The megalithic geek of the trio informed us that West Kennet's status as the longest in Europe was false: at around 350 feet, East Kennet took the laurels. It was at least 5,000 years old, he said, and he had found shards and flints in the ploughland around it.

We left our grids on the nearby bridleway and struck off across the furrows, expecting an angry farmer's shout at any moment. The barrow, shrouded entirely in bushes and trees – its own spinney – was enormous. We crouched by its protruding sarsens at one end, trying to conjure ghosts from the shivery damp. No ghosts came, but instead I had an extraordinary sense of my own mortality. I had never really understood it before, not in my stripling bones, but now they were feeling it as chill fact: I was a mere blip, soon to be extinguished, in comparison with the multiple generations witnessed by this earthwork, and those stretching out into the future. This was possibly my earliest conscious realisation that death was woven into the landscape here in the chalklands in a colossally evident way. I was a bit of a brooder by now, and the Marlborough Downs encouraged you to brood on Last Things, at the same time as they gave you wings.

We searched for ancient treasures on and around the barrow: I kicked at a promising flint and held it out for inspection. Our geek was impressed: 'I think it's an axe head,' he said. It certainly looked like one, bulbous at one end and sharpening to a serrated edge. He advised me to take it back to the Mount House, where a teacher supervised the tiny museum of college finds.

We stood on the edge of the barrow and saw the pudding-bowl lump of Silbury Hill in the distance. Although we'd trooped into the school's Bradleian Theatre for an introductory lecture on the general area in my second term, the current notion of a single and vast 'complex' that might have included Stonehenge twenty miles to the south was never (as far as I remember) mooted: only the immediate area around Avebury was so designated. All I gathered was that no one knew why these things had been thrown up, that they were the debris of former beliefs, and that Merlin and flying saucers had nothing to do with them. I recall a distinct, rather creepy sense of darkness, like a dark fog, as the lecturer – Martin Evans, a genuinely funny history teacher who was to bring a crystal note of humour and kindliness to my time at Marlborough – took us briskly through the Neolithic remnants and their sad destruction at the hands of farmers and fanatics. It was impossible to imagine these sites as they might have looked to their builders, to the peoples of the time: as something brilliantly and gleamingly new and modern (although the 'modern' is itself a modern concept, of course).

Was this swirling gloom during the lecture a product of my sense of alienation, a kind of grief?

In the neglected cupboard drawers of 'A' house basement, where we'd change for games, I had found team photographs dating from the Edwardian period, some sixty years earlier. There was one of the house rugby team in 1910: two rows of boys aged thirteen or fourteen, the perfect age for the trenches when war broke. I was already a Great War obsessive: our English teacher, the old and delightfully eccentric Mr Coggan, brought back from retirement to teach the dunces, had a limp from those same trenches and taught us Sassoon and Owen with a kind of self-therapeutic passion. We liked him so much that when he tested his powers of telepathy on us, we humoured him. 'Banana,' he said, opening his blue eyes. 'Yes, sir, amazing,' I replied. I had been picturing, with vivid precision, an apple.

I would stare at those photos mounted on card, those confident sporty faces, wondering how many had survived. *England expects…*

Oddly, it never occurred to me to see if their names were carved into the great curving inner wall of the Memorial Hall, where the entire school would gather for assemblies or concerts or plays on excruciatingly uncomfortable benches.

Built in 1925, semi-circular, fronted by eight massive stone columns, the 'Mem Hall' was built as a monumental reminder of the 749 old boys prematurely killed by the war: almost the school's total complement at any one time.

Charles Hamilton Sorley's name was up there. Reckoned to be as great a loss to English poetry as Wilfred Owen, Sorley also loved wandering the downs in order to escape 'the prison house of prefectship'. Although his cheery, open nature and excellence at field sports made the school an easier place for him than it was for others, he despised competitiveness and felt the hellish suffering of those who were non-athletic in a system obsessed with sporting achievement and physical prowess, and he particularly rejected speed. Running in the rain brought him closer to a more 'primitive' sense of Nature, so he relished it. This extract from his long schoolboy poem Rain describes what was still known as a 'sweat' sixty years later: a cross-country run given as punishment, preferably early in the morning when cold, windy and wet.

There is something in the rain
That would bid me to remain:
There is something in the wind
That would whisper, "Leave behind
All this land of time and rules,
Land of bells and early schools.
Latin, Greek and College food
Do you precious little good.
Leave them: if you would be free
Follow, follow after me!"

The hall was part of the school's very own death complex, being connected to the Chapel by a stone walkway and including a 'pool of remembrance' in front (now a flower bed) and, beyond a brick loggia, the cosy Rose Garden with its mournful Greek inscription:

Within this quiet garden-close
Though o'er all lands our graves lie spread,
Still do we live and walk with those
Whose thoughts are with the dead.

In other words, the garden was thronged with phantoms. Lucky, perhaps, that no one translated it for us at the time.

It was in the Mem Hall, in my third term, during the dreaded Monday morning assembly, that I heard about the death of a new friend. The Master, in wavery tones, announced that a 'serious accident' had taken place on the weekend Outward Bound trip to Snowdon. Timothy, who sat next to me in French, was exceptional in that he was both clever and nice, his kind smile and civilised words beginning to brighten my days: our friendship was in the budding phase. I had had lunch with him and another friend in Norwood Hall (the huge modern canteen) just before he had set off for the coach in his orange cagoule. In fact, I had wished him luck, feeling a little envious. Now I was sitting among the entire school population – 800 living beings, including many I feared or detested – hearing about his death. He had fallen off the mountain. The Master initially avoided the term 'killed' or even 'death', referring instead to his 'injuries': I had already heard the rumours, broadcast in fragments, that Tim had not got back, that something bad had happened. Then the Master started referring to 'loss' and 'sorrow', that Tim's mother had cancer, and that we had to think especially about his father and sister. By the end I understood. It was as if Tim had died during the time of the announcement.

What was additionally shocking for me, however, was that several of the boys around me were sniggering. Timothy's surname lent itself to a morbid pun. They were whispering and sniggering. At that moment I felt I was trapped in a house of horrors. I don't think I have ever quite recovered from that moment in the vast and oppressive hall of death. It has left me with a residue, not just of grief, but of fear – fear of my fellow human beings. That human beings can, given the right circumstances – an absence of love, say – entirely lack compassion, or feeling. Never mind my more mature rationalisation of that sniggering as a shocked, defensive reaction, a kind of numbing; I see those boys too clearly, and especially one who, short and rotund, a popular target for bullies, seemed to be in paroxysms of glee.

No rituals, no ceremonies, no memorials. No vigils, no flowers, no poems, no counsellors, no nothing. Just the empty desk, the unoccupied bed, his belongings ushered away to join him in oblivion.

I learnt about the details from those in 'A' House who had

been on the expedition. They chatted about it with a kind of swagger. No one, not one pupil, cried: only our French teacher, a tight-lipped and awkward spinster, cracked up when handing back our homework, the desk next to me starkly empty. I wanted to cry – to howl, even – but hid my tears in embarrassment. The details were relentless: Timothy had somehow stumbled off the path and slid down a glacier while walking up the mountain with the others. Although the sports teacher had yelled at him to use his ice-axe, he'd kept knocking the ice with the handle instead of the blade. Then he had vanished from sight over a six-hundred-foot precipice. To alert the emergency services in those pre-mobile days, the sports teacher ran four miles without stopping. He returned to his lessons with a glazed look and eventually had a nervous breakdown and left for good.

Had there been a fatal moment of horseplay near the edge? Tim was at the back of the group, the teacher was leading from the front. Vertiginous drops attract boys, they pretend to push each other over, dare one another: this hadn't been a drop but a gradual, glacial slope to a drop. One cheery scuffle, boots skidding on the ice… Something, anyway, had gone wrong. Tim losing his balance. The gentle slope of the glacier taking him on its sheer slipperiness slowly to the six-hundred foot drop, as the others watched disbelieving and the young sports teacher yelled.

And I'm still yelling with him, yelling into the fierce cold and the wind.

Four

Such memories remain like tiny hard nodules in the general mass, obliterated only on the outside by further layers.

A tell of oblivion, full of lost stories.

Or a mnemonic hulk in case the gods forget.

Tim was only the first: our 1970 intake was to see eleven others follow him over the next twelve years: given that the total of new boys and girls in that year was around 150, this is a remarkably high attrition rate. Accident, murder, suicide, illness… in 1982, when I was back there for a year as a beak, mourning the eleventh – a close friend who had killed himself a week earlier – the new Master confided in me that he thought my year was 'cursed'. Some weeks later, a girl from the same intake was murdered in Thailand. Only recently, one I remember fondly (quiet and sensitive) drove to Marlborough from his home some eighty miles away and hanged himself from an ancient oak in Savernake Forest, depriving the impoverished of a caring, committed GP.

And it was our friend Ray, artist and volunteer fireman, who was designated to cut him down. Sometimes the threads in life tangle and knot.

It pays, in adolescence, not to face that horde…

And under the memory bank? Was there ever a time when the space was virgin?

Before Silbury there was a gentle slope, common-or-garden land: a chalk spur subsiding to a moist, river-meandered valley to the north, the ridge of a long hill to the east. Flints were knapped, hazelnuts cooked, maybe the odd pig slaughtered and eaten. The ordinary traffic of the everyday. Or not quite: according to Jim Leary, who led the latest excavations from 2007 to 2008 as part of the massive salvage and conservation project, the whole area was 'a hive of activity'. The monuments and constructions that were already present – the Windmill Hill enclosure and the long barrows were already a millennium old – kept being added to, with the henges and avenues expanding, great timber posts and huge sarsens going up, the old stuff being demolished, new stuff erected. He interprets the 'thin, grey band of silty clay' free of stones – the original Neolithic ground level under Silbury – as heavily trampled subsoil, the grassy surface having been stripped and cleared of its sarsens. Trampled by the traffic of feet: feet determined to create a flat building surface, or pounding to the rhythm of goatskin drums? A burnt area might indicate more than the final stage of what anthropologists call a 'subsistence strategy' (cooking): it might be the remains of a ceremonial hearth. A fire around which the people danced.

Conjecture.

But then something definite happened: a new hill, a hand-made hill, began.

It began as a nodule. Gravel was brought, possibly from the river, and dumped on the toe of the spur to make a shallow mound about 30 feet in diameter. This gravel must have been special, although there were other tumps (made of dark mud and turves) within the hill's eventual circumference.

Leary described the gravel as 'sticky', 'dull' and 'golden' when he reached it at the end of the old 1849 tunnel, as Richard Atkinson had reached it forty years earlier. I have a flint on my desk that I picked up on Knap Hill, a huge causewayed enclosure not far from Avebury: the stone contains the memory of a lone walk, a certain moment in the chalklands. It is both a lump of flint and a talisman. I have a litter of such stones, as many people do. The gravel was doubtless not just gravel.

When I try to imagine this earliest phase, I can't shake off the Bath Road. A raised track following the drier spur through a river valley prone to bogginess or flooding. Maybe there was always a path there, a kind of broad badger-trail, tracks being conservative things. What we do know, from the lack of remains, is that ordinary daily activity – cooking, eating, washing up – was not conducted on the site once the first mounds had marked it.

Then construction proceeded by leaps and bounds, although how long between each leap remains unknown, and the word 'proceeded' might be misleading. A ring of stakes was knocked in around the gravel cairn and fresh turves laid on, followed by a slew of marshy soil, chalk and more coloured flinty bits, this reaching waist-high and, in cross-section, looking somewhat like a dark compost heap layered with the yellow gravel and brown clay. One amateur researcher, Colin Berry, suggests the 'organic' material could be human innards placed there in a process of ritual evisceration, making Silbury 'a communal organ reliquary'. Whether grisly or not, this 'organic' turf stack has preserved its grassland insects intact, having been cut from a wide area around the stripped site: a squashed leaf beetle, in the wrong place at the wrong time, still shows its iridescent wing-cases in a clod of turf; snail shells are in perfect condition, as if newly-buried; fragments of moss and grass curl as they would in a picnic sandwich, along with bramble seeds, yew berries, hazel shells, nettle seeds and so on caught in the thick mats of soil. A whole landscape spreads before us: mature, well-grazed grassland amidst small woods, with the odd patch of corn and glimmers of reedy wetland. According to the English Heritage report, no other burial mound of the period has revealed such a 'managed' pastoral context: 'it is simply unique'. Cows, pigs, sheep and goats. Some cultivated plots, but nothing permanent, as these people were seasonally or annually mobile – albeit keeping within a certain range, a certain landscape, heading not too far into the wild or some possibly hostile territory. Herders, with simple thatched dwellings, easy to make or mend. Barking of large, semi-feral dogs through the smoke: guarding, warning, fending off. Much of the country was still darkly wooded. Watch for those wolves, the massive aurochs, the wild boars that uproot or trample everything with their snouts and hooves. Avoid them, they'll avoid you. Unless a young man needs to prove his manhood, his skills, then we'll organise it. The initiation. Not a knotted rope of sheets over a void but a flint-tipped spear against a bull-like creature, almost 6 feet at the shoulder, weighing in at over 2,000 lbs, with long, sharp horns curving forwards so that the tip can be kept within the beast's field of vision. A crash in the thick woods, a dark brown shadow, keeping itself to itself as the woods diminish century after century until there are no aurochs left at all: no bones have been found in Britain dating after 1300 BC. The great totem animal fell with the great woods.

This latest mound's diameter was roughly equal to the length of five aurochs snout to tail – or a large bus. At an unknown point after its construction, narrow pits were dug into it, and the dwarf hill swollen with topsoil, chalk, more gravel, clay and further hods of turf, as well as a few embedded sarsen stones: it was now an impressive 100 feet in diameter and perhaps up to 20 feet high. Already enormous, but the natives were restless.

The ditch was scooped out – perhaps this was done first of all, we can't tell – and its white chalk used to build banks around the mound, gradually expanding it. The monument was now enclosed by a twenty-foot-wide trench, which had a waist-high bank rimming its inner edge. That'll keep the dogs out, or whatever isn't wanted.

A classic causewayed enclosure, in archaeologist's lingo, but with a big bump in the middle, its summit as high as an apple tree.

The ditch does not stay still: rapidly backfilled, it is rechiselled further out and the process repeated, like the expanding rings of an oak. The fifth ditch is the one we see today. Crushed chalk is dumped within girdling hoops or revetments made from lumps of chalk rubble; these walls (angled inwards for stability) proceed up in a series of six ziggurat-like ledges that form a spiral access path. This path is debated, but how else would they have carried up the material in the days before the wheel? A similar spiral is a feature of the aforementioned College Mound in its landscape-garden heyday, presumably appropriating an earlier element that might even have been original. And a spiral exactly mimics cyclical time, the seasons returning a year further on. A progress up the hill would enact the deepest movement of nature, a shape found in the double helix of DNA and in the structures of galaxies – including our own. It is also, of course, one of the commonest motifs in Neolithic petroglyphs.

Silbury is not actually round at the base: like the Globe Theatre, which was considered a proper 'little O' by Shakespeare, but turned out to be a twenty-sided polygon, the round-looking hill has up to nine sides. We have no idea whether the summit was originally flat, or rounded like an egg and then sliced off by the Saxons in Ethelred's time to build their impressive hillfort against the terrifying Danes. The iron bridle-bit unearthed on the summit in 1723, since lost, probably dated from this time. It would seem odd to go to all that trouble and not leave a space at the top for ceremonial purposes, however small. At some point the spiralling gradations were infilled to give her present smooth bowl-shape; back then the hill was, at least initially and for maybe a couple of centuries or more if kept weeded, as white as snow.

Dazzling white, especially when the sun lit it. Or a cold flood of moon.

Nine sides! Mathematics again! It is possible, as with the contemporaneous Egyptian pyramids, that straight-line measurements were made with cords stretched between pegs; it was then a simple step to establish arcs, circles or even to determine a right-angle: tie the ends of two cords to each peg, move the other ends about but keep them taut; mark the two points where the arcs meet and then draw a line between them, which will bisect the original line at a right-angle. But maybe they never needed to take this step. Neither Avebury nor Stonehenge show the millimetric precision and accuracy of the Pyramids; in comparison, they are rough-cuts.

All this hill-building took about a hundred years: the time it took to complete King's College Chapel in Cambridge, from first stone to last pane of stained glass, in the fifteenth and sixteenth centuries.

Dr Jim Leary, whose English Heritage team eventually managed to plug the hole and render Silbury fit again, emptying her of her metal propwork, time capsules, Victorian poems, BBC plaques and general well-meaning litter, surmises that this never-ending tweaking and adjusting – lasting just three or four generations – reflects the importance of 'process' rather than end product: perhaps the bringing and dumping of the different types of soils and stones, the embedded tools and sarsen boulders, had their own ritual meaning. The soil-types do not seem to have been used willy-nilly, but 'thoughtfully selected'. It has to be said that this emphasis on the doing is true of ancient rites and shamanic practice in general. But Silbury was certainly not, as the *Daily Mail* headlined Leary's report, 'an accident'.

Conversely, we might see the different stages as a series of finished projects that successive generations or even different power structures decided to alter or enhance; this being similar to cathedrals like Cologne or Canterbury, which were generally built on the same site and incorporated the earlier buildings, even though the latter were seen as finished.

Yet the idea that she was, after all, a symbolic refuse tip of memories rather than of dreams has its attractions.

But how did the Neolithic regard memory? As something that might be projected into a clod of earth, a flint, an antler pick? For that matter, how did they regard emotion – the emotion of grief, or anger, or fear? Might the hill be a waste

**SILBURY
HILL**

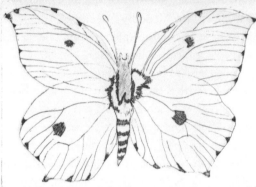

BRIMSTONE

**EMMER
SPIKELET**

Tilson 1976

stack of human feelings, or even a kind of safe storage of some dangerous emotion or impulse? Lucy Lippard's classic book *Overlay: Contemporary Art and the Art of Prehistory* cites an Eskimo custom that offers 'an angry person release by walking the emotion out of his or her system in a straight line across the landscape; the point at which the emotion is conquered is marked with a stick, bearing witness to the strength or length of the rage.' The stick, led up to by the line of footprints in the snow, remains a visible trace, a homeopathic depositing, not only of the final mastering but of the rage itself. A Line Made By Anger.

If Leary is right about the different soils being full of meaning – geographical, mythological, religious – then Silbury becomes a kind of book, or library, packed with words and images. A library that could not be physically opened or entered. Or even like a shoebox full of old family snaps, the lid never to be lifted. The words, the stories, the memories, were preserved in people's heads, in minds that have now crumbled to soil's constituent molecules. We understand it as little as they would have understood a bound volume of Shakespeare, a big fat Bible – or a heap of creased snapshots.

If that really was the case, however, might we not expect to find more elaborate or sophisticated mementoes from these people? Axes, gold jewellery, copper swords and knives, fine pots, even incisions on bone? As we find in their tombs? The language of memory here seems impoverished in comparison to the great statement of its form and structure, but maybe that is only because we have lost the code. We cannot decipher what was written in gesture, oral speech, invisible and unrecorded urgings.

Maybe, in 5,000 years, surviving humans will again be

casting their clods and turves of stories and myths to build up their great earthern library, and the written word will be a mysterious squiggle, like the mark of disease on a leaf.

Ink squiggles on paper caused much excitement in 2010, when letters from Edward Drax (he of the vertical shaft) were discovered in the British Library by Brian Edwards, a local historian. Drax is describing the excavations to Lord Rivers, and includes a tantalising detail about a 'perpendicular cavity' reached by the miners 95 feet down: it was six inches across. 'We have already followed it about 20 feet, we can plumb it about Eleven feet more.' This suggests a hole left by organic material, most likely a wooden pole if taken together with later accounts of Drax having found oak fragments. A very tall, quite slender post subsequently buried in the heightening of the mound suggests either a measuring pole to keep the central point in view, or a totem pole, or even a kind of sun-dial style that cast a significant shadow. If it was a post.

Sometimes that's all memory is: the solid original reduced to the report of its absence. A verbal ghost trace.

Meanwhile, my own memories suddenly change colour. Although the downs were a refuge, my heart was still in the clear-floored Buckinghamshire beechwoods – less bleak, and where home was. Then, in my second school year, my parents moved to West-Central Africa: Pan Am had posted my father to Douala, the main port of Cameroon. With its hot-flannel humidity, its pot-holes, its shanties, its insect-caked swimming pools, its colour and noise, its hammering rain in the rainy season (unfortunately coinciding with the summer holidays), even its local Printania supermarket with limbless beggars in front, nothing could have been more different from either Chesham or Marlborough.

Mangrove swamps along the glittery river's estuary, thick forest or 'bush' cut through by roads of red earth littered with car wrecks, a big volcano and a small volcano, long deserted beaches of black laval sand washed by white-frothed combers, misty highlands and savannah in the north, gorillas in the south, a broader variety of flora and fauna than anywhere else in the world, charcoal-smelling villages of thatched mud-huts where the inhabitants would wave and shout 'White man!' as we bumped past in our rusty company Peugeot or friend's Land Rover, it all seemed – it was – impossibly exotic.

I already knew the country through Gerald Durrell's wildlife books, to which I had been addicted, and had an unfocussed passion for animals. In one sense, I couldn't quite believe that my father had been posted to Cameroon, of all countries, as I had been dreaming of it for years. My friends were not that interested: unlike India or Nepal, Africa was completely unhip in the early 1970s.

I had caught her proverbial bug in the Congo in 1967 during one of my father's brief tours out there, despite it coinciding with a violent uprising.

Moving to Douala during term-time, Dad sent back postcards of Hotel Akwa, which had a 'nice swimming pool'. I stared at it secretly in my senior house: being caught with something that looked precious to you was dangerous. I flew out finally with my mother and sister, proud of my new portable tape recorder and a collection consisting of two tapes (Strawbs and Neil Young's *Harvest*) recorded with a microphone off a friend's speakers – the traffic from the Bath Road clearly audible underneath.

3/5/66

AVION

It is nicer here
than I expected. Not
excessively hot & the
town is pleasant
compared with Calcutta.
The restaurants are
good too. The green
blots on the river
are plants, which
grow so fast they
sometimes interfere
with shipping. Love

RETURNING ON 16 —

Mrs E. A. THORPE,
"WITCH-HAZEL",
WYEDALE VIEW,

BAKEWELL,
DERBYSHIRE,
ANGLETERRE

The shock of the humid air, clamped against your face the moment you stepped out of the plane, triggered the surprise of tears. How could I think of living here, when the air itself was like an alien medium, a kind of warm and invisible liquid that needed aquatic lungs? The modest airport was full of yelling men in tatty teeshirts scrambling for luggage, and a few large women wrapped in multi-coloured cloth shouting at them with equal fervour. The odour of sweat-clamped bodies was, for some reason, agreeable. 'Organised chaos,' murmured my father, slapping at a mosquito on his cheek.

Despite having imbibed the period's unthinking post-colonial racism, our two months in Kinshasa when I was ten had accustomed me to being in a (white) minority, and so I was unfazed by the blackness of everybody else's skin; the saturated air, however, brought home a change that was no longer a fantasy but the vivid truth, sharp as the quinine I had to take against malaria.

My bedroom walls were so moist that none of my posters would stay up – not even my prize one of Marc Bolan in a silver jump-suit. The Pan Am flat was on the ground floor of one of the two modest tower blocks in Douala, and had no air-conditioning, just a fan in the sitting room. There was no television, and radio was local, Mount Cameroon blocking out the World Service to a murmuring hiss. Each day the kids would come to the balcony with their drums, masks and rattles, jittering about for a few thrown centimes.

That was about it for home-grown entertainment, apart from a few vinyls, so the ex-pat community organised, along with pool parties and dinners, alcohol-fuelled film showings from rattly projectors (they all seemed to star Goldie Hawn, the spitting image of the US Vice-Consul's bubbly and bored young wife, on whom I had a crush).

I made a few good friends out of those roughly my age, and my sister and I spent most of the time swimming or reading or listening to records or just larking about: at weekends my father would drive us two hours through the bush to our favourite deserted beach, an endless stretch of mahogany-dark laval sand that I still think of as a semi-mythical place, although quite real enough to try to drown me one time in a breaker's vicious rip. An uncomplicated existence in a place that made England feel small, peevish and grey, until my senses had adjusted to her subtle nuances, her smaller-scale perfections.

Soon we moved to a larger, cooler flat with a view of Mount Cameroon looming over the estuary: liable at any time to spit fire and molten lava, she was an explosive Silbury, cloaked in sub-tropical forest and so high she was brushed with snow on the summit.

In fact, everything natural in Cameroon appeared bigger than its English equivalent. The leaves, the insects, the sunsets, the animals, the waves; even the smells were stronger – everything mouldering in the humidity and heat, charcoal smoke a constant background tang, body sweat clamping tattered tee-shirts or varnishing naked breasts, the murmuring of drums a constant tinnitus, and the air saturated with what took life apart as much as with life itself: perhaps they were one and the same, life and death, because here the process of decomposition was visible and intrinsic. There was always a multitude of insects, devouring, cleaning up, millions of tiny refuse collectors. It was all much slower – the way people walked, the straight-backed women with a jar perched freely on their heads swaying with great elegance slowly and assuredly along the pot-holed roads – but at the same time it was all being ushered along into oblivion.

'The armpit of Africa', said the one old surviving hand from colonial times, chuckling as the sweat trickled through his white stubble, 'has only one remedy: pink gin.'

My London grandmother would join us occasionally, sharing a bedroom with her teenage granddaughter. What did it mean to my sister and me, this temporary relocation among kin, this passing consolidation of the nuclear family, this one-third of the year back among our blood-lines, our begetters, in a humid fug of heat and sheer cultural difference?

Everything that happens to you goes into the heaped-up mass. It all has consequences.

We would fly back to England at the end of every holiday and face the diminutive reality, the greyness and the cold, the colours drained, the streets polished and orderly, and each endure the sentence of term in our separate schools (my sister's the kind that screamed at you if your socks were too short or your skirt not precisely the right shade). It took time to adjust, but at least I was no longer starting off with a psychosomatic spell in the empty school sanatorium – the only patient in the huge ward, consuming endless numbers of *Punch* from the 1950s, dipping my thermometer in my cup of tea and acting feverish.

Slowly the downland would spread its secretive, subtler charms around me again. I stumbled on the naturalist Richard Jefferies' books in the school library. Jefferies, born near Swindon and a favourite of Sorley's, put into words what I was feeling when I walked or biked out.

> From the blue hill lines, from the dark copses on the ridges, the shadows in the combes, from the apple-sweet wind and rising grasses, from the leaf issuing out of the bud to question the sun – there comes from all of these an influence which forces the heart to lift itself in earnest and purest desire.

I am not so sure that my desire was pure, as there were girls in the sixth form and my voice was breaking, but fecund nature made it all seem good, anyway.

And I was happier at school. Writing stories and poems had always been something that had felt natural to me, as had acting (despite shyness), and suddenly these became elements that muted the repeated 'Mr Average' snarl in the echoey house bathrooms. Writing and acting, I could become someone else. Up on stage, slipping on another skin, putting on a permitted mask, I was finding my place as a performer – earning respect, building confidence, making friends, my marks improving in tandem. The bullies and manipulators were now looking up beyond the footlights: I had a new power that grew with each appearance, that came over me with the make-up, the final puff of talc, that sweet smell of make-believe, the heroic trickle of sweat under the hot lights.

Strange transformation, from Mr Average to Mr Actor. I began to be left alone, especially in my 'O' level year, when I wandered quite by chance into the last audition for James Elroy Flecker's *Hassan* (directed by his grandson, a teacher at the school) and landed the title role opposite the *belle* of the sixth form in the year above, the girl who flickered smiles about her like pockets of oxygen, who had a reputation and smelt of French cigarettes. She was expelled three weeks into rehearsals, too late for me not to feel it as a blow to my heart in the blissful rush of rehearsals, of taking the Golden Road to Samarkand time and again out of old Baghdad, of finally defeating the Memorial Hall's deathliness with the command of those hundreds of faces dim beyond the lights.

Eywallah! Eywallah! Know, Selim, that I am in love.

Theatre. A stage. Drama. The drama of ritual. The power. The desire.

So a life builds up in layers, piecemeal, a kind of haphazard engineering that has elements of skill and cunning – the previous layers mostly hidden, as are the smaller mounds within, the clumps of different-coloured earth, the burnt offerings, the nodules of pain and the delight. The hard graft of the chopped-off antlers, picking and stabbing and scraping. The embers of old fires, old flames, in mute fragments of charcoal.

How telling these fragile memories can be.

Recently Jim Leary supervised the coring of the Mound at the heart of the school, taking samples to establish its age for the first time. From top to bottom (it is just over half the height of Silbury), the drills bored down in two different places and extracted four samples of carbonised wood. These charcoal bits tell us that the Mound was begun around 2400 BC: at 4,400 years old, it turns out to be the same age as Silbury just five or so miles up the Bath Road. We have no idea why these two monumental hills were begun at roughly the same time, their construction continuing over several generations. There was a third in the area, within vast Marden Henge, said to be almost as high as the Mound, but it collapsed as it was being excavated by Sir Richard Colt Hoare and William Cunnington in 1807. Interestingly, Hoare – perhaps as a result of the Marden disaster – was an early advocate of a tombless Silbury: 'There can be no doubt that it was one of the component parts of the grand temple at Abury, not a sepulchral mound raised over the bones and ashes of a king or arch-druid.'

Perhaps each false hill was a rival to the other: mine's bigger than yours. And the Marden and Mound clans simply threw in the ox-bone trowel, at some point. OK, guys, we get the message. It's not winning that counts, anyway.

I do recall the Mound being seen as a kind of dwarf Silbury, of course, in the dim and distant 1970s, but a report as recent as 2001 concluded that 'in the absence of data to the contrary, the available archaeological and documentary evidence indicates that the mound is essentially a medieval construction.'

How certain science always sounds! But the 'data to the contrary' was produced, meagre though it was, and suddenly the Mound has become of international importance – joining the other monuments inscribed in 1986 on the UNESCO

World Heritage list as 'Stonehenge, Avebury and Associated Sites'. A headache for the College authorities, no doubt, given their previous treatment, but also a chance to make amends. A surviving snippet of the Marden mound – known as the Hatfield Barrow – has been dated to the same period: a time when, at Stonehenge, the first great stones were being levered upright. Far away, in Mesopotamia, the teeming cities of Sumer and an intricate irrigation system and the first writing system had already been flourishing for hundreds of years, while in Egypt the oldest pyramid, the Pyramid of Cheops, had already been thrusting its 500 feet of high-precision stone blocks into the sun-filled sky for over a century. In India, the influence of Mesopotamian trade was transforming the local culture in the north-west into the highly developed and primarily urban Indus civilisation, with its priest-kings, nose ornaments and home bathrooms. In China, the people of the Longshan culture along the Yellow River were spinning silk and crafting highly polished black pots. Europe had to await the peak of Minoan Crete to be this advanced, but the latter was well underway when the great mounds and rough-hewn circles were going up in a misty island to the north.

Here is what was recovered by the second core from near or on the original ground level of this dorm-shadowing mass of marl, and which plunged it backwards in time into Neolithic clarity and out of a Merlinish mist of uncertainty:

0.013 grams of mature deciduous oak charcoal
0.084 grams of hawthorn, crab apple, whitebeam or other charcoal
0.056 of hazel charcoal
an earthworm egg
one indeterminate insect fragment
a fragment of moss stem

an indeterminate seed
two fragments of calcined bone
one piece of unburnt cortical bone
a fragment of unburnt cancellous bone
five small flint flakes showing signs of knapping

For my part, I had always felt in my own green bones that
the Mound was prehistoric: far too mysterious, too looming
a thing, too dark and enigmatic, to be nothing more than a
dull motte under a Norman keep. We had to walk around its
great bulk every day, it cast the area around it into gloom, its
effect exaggerated by the trees and bushes that used it as their
earth-ball, probing its depths with their roots. The 1960s Art
School block looked straight out through plate glass onto its
eastern slopes a few yards away across a gravel footpath: a

wall of light-speckled dark green, a kind of verdant waterfall
entirely blocking the view. Modern and ancient cheek-by-
jowl, and the ancient always dominant, despite the smell of
turps and ink and paints and glue, the chatter of the arty

types, the classical music that helped to create an ambience.

There was much that swirled about in between those two temporal extremes. Recovered Roman coins suggested a Roman fort; the Normans built a wooden tower on top, then a keep in stone that dominated their impressive castle, spread at the foot of the Mound, where a succession of kings stayed – including bad King John who liked to hunt in Savernake Forest. The castle's stout walls tumbled into heaps of rubble, but the Mound's height was useful during the Civil War.

Peace came, and the hill, described by Sir Robert Moray in 1664 as 'a Auncient Tumulus' with a 'handsomely gravelled' walk and a 'pretty green' at the top set to fruit trees, was now the fashionable main feature in the picturesque garden of the Seymours. The latest Seymour, the sixth Duke of Somerset, demolished the old house and gave the new one to his son, Lord Hertford. This attractive manor was to become a mere coaching inn and then, in the 1840s, the poshest element in a new charitable school for the sons of vicars. (The building's comfortable grandiosity must be an essential selling point, now that the school is for the seriously rich and the genuinely royal.)

None of these afflictions tamed the shaggy monster, its late picturesqueness added to by Lady Hertford with a fashionable grotto scooped from the base and encrusted with shells. Grottoes were a link with the pagan past, albeit a classical one: natural caves originally dedicated to water nymphs in Greek and Roman times, the neo-classical version revived a relationship with nature that Christian belief had desiccated.

Lady Hertford liked to have a personal poet in residence during the summer. In William Kent and Nicolas-Henry

Tardieu's illustration to 'Spring' in James Thomson's *The Seasons*, the celebrated poem part-written in the grounds, we see an exaggerated Mound and, in the distance, an impressive peak probably inspired by Silbury. Lady Hertford liked to

dress up as an Arcadian shepherdess with her friends, and may have served as the model for the personification of Spring draped in the foreground. Her guests would have begun the spiral walk up her very own Parnassus (under the aegis of its

Druidic resident, Merlin) with a pause in the grotto – a dark, mysterious, even suggestive cave trickling with water drawn from the summit of a hill described by another of Hertford's poets, Stephen Duck, as a 'Mountain'. ('Here often round the verdant Plain I stray,/Where Thomson sung his bold, unfetter'd Lay;/Or climb the winding, mazy Mountain's Brow.') No one climbed mountains at this period, thus the walk up may have seemed impressive to a man in a knee-length coat, frilly shirt, silk stockings and stacked heels. And from the summit, as Daniel Defoe noted in 1724, 'you look over [a] great part of the town'.

Duck himself was born into a family of dirt-poor labourers in the nearby Pewsey valley, and bettered himself through reading, eventually accepted into high society as a rare example of a 'natural' genius – particularly when his startling poem on the hard grind of agricultural work, *The Thresher's Labour*, was published. I like the idea of him straddling the two worlds, wandering the gravel walks of Lord and Lady Hertford's ornamental Eden with its 'beauteous Grot' and real-life 'lovely nymphs', yet with his memories still intact of 'the rattling sound' of the whirling flails, when your body trickled with 'briny Streams', the 'Sweat, the Dust, and suffocating Smoak' blackening your face so that your children shrieked when you came home.

Waft it all away.

He eventually drowned himself, this brilliantly successful, witty and gifted man. Perhaps he fell into the gap between the two worlds. Perhaps being a 'natural' in a highly artificial society was too much of a strain. It was to turn John Clare, the other (greater) 'natural' genius, insane.

William Stukeley, also a frequent guest, drew a bird's-eye view of the house and grounds in 1723: we see a neat, spiral-stepped 'Mount' topped by a summer house and a cleaned-up ditch circling the base, full of water that feeds into a long and narrow fishpond. Stukeley noted the number

of springs welling up in the ditch: what was called the Moat in my day, a survival of the Norman castle's defences and the subsequent fishpond, was still fed by the springs: the Moat stayed icy cold even in the summer.

This was the school swimming pool, alas – and a lure for our sadistic P.E. teacher in my first year, a huge Australian called Murray, who chose especially wintry days to use it for lessons. When he forced our classmate David to jump in, or rather pushed him in, on the basis that a non-swimmer would rather swim than drown, and the basis proved mistaken, I was ordered to dive in and pull him out. I did so, aware that my friend was already underwater in the deep end, but he proved heavy, and a panicked arm, slippery as a tentacle, was wrapped around my neck: I all but saw my thirteen years of life pass before my eyes.

Giving one last effort, I felt the concrete side under my hand. Everyone cheered. After dressing in the open-air changing rooms, blue-lipped with cold, half the class went off to the Sanatorium suffering from serious exposure. Murray was given the push himself, to general relief, and apparently went back to warmer climes.

The Moat of painful memory is now gone – at least, I couldn't find it a few years ago, lost among the new state-of-the-art buildings in that corner. As a pupil I would sometimes come across a greying Old Boy trying to find his bearings, muttering about change and progress, and suddenly I was him. It didn't seem possible. It's not the same place! Did I ever board here? My dreams know I boarded here – burrowing down, coring my unconscious and bringing up incoherent fragments, indeterminate seeds, knapped flakes. Sorrow and joy.

Nowhere is the same place. Even Silbury changes. Or rather, we change.

Merlin's Mound, a pagan-Christian hybrid, was allowed to dwindle in the nineteenth century to something wilder, messier – more out of neglect than environmental concern, although the water tank on the summit was pure Victorian vandalism. Trees rooted and grew taller. It became a kind of steep-sloped spinney. The grotto had a lot of its shells nicked and became a crumbling, dank den for smokers and bikes: that's how I remember it, anyway. The nymphs had long departed. Whether they have returned with the grotto's recent restoration is a moot point.

In 1912, the College built their boiler-house and dug an

insensitive groove into one flank to house the brick flue; Mr H.C. Brentnall, a teacher at the school and an amateur archaeologist, recovered six red-deer antlers during the works. He surmised they were Neolithic in origin, and not trophies from King John's hunts in Savernake Forest: in his report he wrote that 'three of these fragments consist of the burr and broken brow-tine, and two others seem to be consecutive portions of the beam of the antler to which one of the brow tines belonged.' The burr is the bulbous root of the antler, the brow tine is the lowest branch off the main beam, the pair either side sticking forward like horns – popular these days for key rings. And 4,000 or more years ago? Did the tines' phallic look mean they had special status? Did Mr H.C. Brentnall know what he was suggesting when he went on to write 'it is unlikely that the fragments… thoroughly impregnated with chalk' could have been buried after 'the erection of the mound'. Did he even know he was writing a kind of Heaneyesque poetry *avant la lettre*?

> The burr and broken brow-tine,
> the beam of the antler –
> impregnated with chalk
> through the mound's erection.

Jon Cannon, historian of sacred spaces, climbed it recently. According to his blog, he found 'at the top, some brickwork and a tank, and the words *Lavinia and Adam made love here.*' Honest, I only climbed it once, at night, without permission, to puff on a cigarette with my mates. None of them was called Lavinia. But whoever that couple were, and if it wasn't just braggadocio, they might well have been reviving a sacred, very serious tradition.

Sex, the experts assume, was an integral part of whatever rituals took place here and on Silbury. Tiny phallic objects – erect penises in chalk and thighs opened with an incised groove – have been recovered from causewayed enclosures like nearby Windmill Hill. And so have what are possibly the bones of sacrificial victims: as mentioned earlier, the Kennet Avenue, that great line of stones leading out of Avebury

for one-and-a-half miles towards Waden Hill and Silbury, has many burials, mostly unaccompanied by artefacts, at key points beside or even under a stone. They were interred when the sarsens in question were in the process of being installed: an adult male with cuts to his legs; a small child; a muddle of bones belonging to two teenagers, and many more such deposits to help the avenue's potency. What pottery was found with them is not local; some of it is Beaker. Prisoners? Vulnerable strangers? Or influential immigrants whose kin thought they deserved the monument's aura, and who happened to be present as the stones were being erected?

Sex. Death. Fertility.

For one friend at least, the Mound was the site of the opposite: a scientific experiment. Was I in the same Physics set as Paul? If so, I have obliterated that afternoon lesson. Or maybe I was ill with 'flu in Sanny, alone in a long ward where Victorian boys had snuffled and died in the iron beds. 'We weighed ourselves,' said Paul, 'and calculated the height of the Mound via trigonometry. We could then calculate our horsepower from the time it took to move our respective mass up to the top: don't ask me the formula now as that didn't stick; what sticks is a sense of excitement, of being outside during lessons and the feeling of a damp late afternoon in early October or March. It was more fun than the usual lesson, as the Mound was out of bounds to us.'

So much for the objectivity of science. So much for theories of education: what sticks is the poetry of sensed experience, good or bad. The icy slap of wintry water, the leaf-mould sweetness of the fresh outdoors when everyone else is in class or in Chapel (which I skipped regularly to go walking). The formula, what was the formula? The formulas run our lives, after all, concocting the way we live. Hedged in by science and technology, what choices do we have? New tinkered-with molecules swirl in our veins as the plastic junk swirls in the Pacific. Paul remembers the sweetness of the air, the forbidden sight of the Mound's summit. But not the formula.

The formulas are certainly there in Jim Leary's report on

the Mound excavations, detailing radiocarbon measurements: impossible clusters of numbers and letters (T' = 0.9, T' (5 per cent) = 3.8, v = 1) under which those few charcoal fragments have vanished, or have been transfigured.

What a journey that charred hazel twig has undertaken – a Pooh Stick on the river of time – since it first flared into black on some modest fire kindled in that shallow river valley, on its moist and misty gravels, its silty clay, for a purpose none of us can know! For simple warmth, perhaps, as with the fire that the guards with their bows and arrows sat around cheerfully all night long in our Congo garden, chatting and drinking as the darkness sizzled with insects and the giant moths fluttered and flared. (How comforting those guards were, despite their virtual defencelessness.) Or for some lost sacred purpose – flame near water, the scorching of ancestral bones, heat in the sharp cold furring the weather-browned faces as the eyes shone and sparkled. Was it day or night? Were charms spoken? Was anyone or anything sacrificed? Could they imagine the Mound soon to cover that space in which they sat back on their heels and watched, coughing in the smoke?

No evidence. No data. Certainly no great mass of marl as yet: just a shallow river valley and the sound of trickling springs, their chill subterranean water, puffs of hazel and whitebeam and oak and hawthorn as far as the eye could see. The good river (the good Kennet, ancient and suggestive name) shallow itself over stones. Murmuring voices, odd bursts of laughter, dogs and children and women, women at chores and the men – what did the men do? They were now tied to their cows, pigs, sheep and goats and to the soil, no longer mere hunters padding light of foot through woods after flickering beasts, but bargaining with clods and furrows, with frost and drought, fist-deep in the careful management of animals.

The Neolithic revolution that changed humanity less than 10,000 years ago, emerging in the Fertile Crescent – from modern-day Iran and through Iraq to Turkey – has been seen as both a good thing and a bad thing, like the Industrial Revolution that is its only equivalent. But these people in the river valley, staring into the fire, have no memory of the hunter-gatherer time, unless it has survived as piecemeal myth or fragments of unquestioned ritual. They hunt only for symbolic purposes, or as proof of male prowess, keeping the spear arm in trim for tribal conflicts, or for the odd taste of game when the need arises. The smoke billows up into the usual grey, the low English ceiling of cloud, black smudges on grey. Or vanishes into the moon-pearled levels of night cloud, or the clear stars some of them can read.

And from this world of scratch farmers and their herds and their cosy thatched dwellings there rode that hazel twig out of the dying embers, to be heaped over with turf, buried under 50-odd feet of earth, travelling on its long voyage into a laboratory, a machine none of us but a tiny elite can comprehend or explain. A voyage spent mostly in clamped darkness, near an earthworm egg, hundreds of decades of darkness and silence until the metal drill-bit came, coring time like an apple.

Five

A charred hazel twig. Or a complete person!
An embarrassment of riches.

Last year I travelled to the South Tyrol Museum of Archaeology in Bolzano, Italy, to meet Ötzi, or the Ice Man, face to face... because his face survives, complete with eyeballs (his eyes were brown). His frozen, mummified remains, along with his clothes and tools and accessories, were discovered on a high mountain pass by walkers in 1991. He died of an arrow wound and a head injury – murdered, in other words – at least 700 years before Silbury was begun.

He is Neolithic, but his fur cap might have been made yesterday; there are sweat marks on his stitched clothes, he has a quiver full of arrows and a backpack and birchbark pots and soot-blackened lungs from squatting by open fires. Threaded onto his belt were two pieces of birch fungus known to have antibiotic properties and his staring right eye still has an eyelash and his leggings were repatched many times. His cow-leather shoes are stuffed with straw, in which he walks into our lives as a living being caught and preserved at a single moment – the last – in his life. He is not a skeleton laid after death in a tomb with his grave belongings settled around him, but a man caught unawares who – judging from the injuries to his right hand – fought against a thrusting blade to preserve that life, and whose belongings have tumbled about him.

But what was it that moved me most of all in this museum, so I was swallowing back the tears?

The knots.

These were *his* knots: they show his thought, his care, even his imagination. This was a man from times when everything carried – apart from the copper axe – was pre-technological. You were self-sufficient, but your bargain was with nature. Flint, wood, grass, hide, fur, plants, feathers, antlers, birch tar, fibres, tree bast, tinder fungus, bone, bark, leaves. These were what sustained Ötzi and his Neolithic contemporaries. Their needs were easier to satisfy, their carbon footprint was minimal, their perspective was coupled to experience and the senses. 'Life is given us,' wrote Schopenhauer, 'not to be enjoyed, but to be overcome – to be got over.' They knew adversity, with their toothache and their joint pain and their old wounds, and yet they faced it with their knots and their natural paraphernalia and their cunning and their little bags of this and that. And they still wanted to build impossible temples.

For me, it was a revelation. Although Ötzi had been lying in the ice for many hundreds of years before the first turf stack was put into place, the first sarsen lifted, I now think of the builders of Silbury and Avebury as people, not as ghostly mysteries or supermen or magicians or even as vague forms smoked from foetal skeletons. It was the knots that did it. And his torn, dangling chinstraps.

Individuals.

Yet I imagine the lone mind as blurred into its environment, steeped in the tribe or the clan or the communal energy and immersed in what we now label, because there's an alternative to it, the natural world; the body itself stinking of the natural, like something encrusted, the leather and furs (woven cloth not yet quite known in northern Europe) stiff and stained with sweat, the lungs with wood-smoke – and the very movements of the sinewy limbs reflecting this: where not crippled by the rigours of a life of constant survival, they would still be slow and strong and graceful. A total dependence on what lay around and about, no hospitals or social services or state aid. No state. Nothing to fall back on but the communal energy, whose smallest unit was the clan. Periods perhaps on the edge of famine, or buffeted by extreme weather – drought, severe cold, flood.

According to Aubrey Burl in his still-unsurpassed *Prehistoric Avebury*, the examination of period burials reveals, not only a ghastly catalogue of ways to suffer and die (plenty of fractures and wounds, severe arthritis, tooth abscesses, gum disease, rickets, polio, spina bifida, tetanus, tuberculosis, plague, malaria), but the likelihood that 'four people in ten died before they were twenty' – not including the 50 per cent who didn't make it past their third year.

When an archaeologist in a recent BBC documentary on Silbury suggested that these people led simple, self-sufficient but quite comfortable lives in their sparsely-populated landscape, I felt the gust of whimsy in a contemporary context of general fuck-up. What about the diseases? The crippling damp? The animal and human predators lurking in the shadows? But I felt I knew what she meant: clusters of thatched dwellings in rich grazing dotted with cows and sheep, pigs fattening free in the woods, a lot of juniper-scattered scrubland, untouched forest beyond, small unintensive fields of corn, a lot of silence, a lot of nature, no cities, no factory farms, no traffic, no piped-in rubbish filling their heads.

Instead of jingles, songbirds – more than you could ever imagine. A lot more snuffling hedgehogs. Badgers, who just got on with it as they always have done. Space to breathe. Soil and rivers not doped in synthetic molecules, not tainted by liquids and powders and pellets with names as ugly as their chemical smell. I know about that smell: one summer vacation I helped a farmer spray his near-ripe wheat, holding up a ladder beyond the brow to give him a sightline. Neolithic settlements would have smelt, but with a strong and delicious pungency – of smoke and straw and animal skins and cooking on an open fire and a kind of nuttiness, with a hint of rotted-down dung and sweat. 'Feeling the cool wind of the night and smelling the good smell of Africa,' Hemingway wrote, 'I was altogether happy.'

The Silver Age.

The Silver Age, because the Golden Age was pre-farming – the Palaeolithic and then the (transitional) Mesolithic: the small hunting groups would be generally on the move, with plenty of free game, fish, hazelnuts and fruit to go round: as Neil Oliver cagily puts it in *A History of Ancient Britain*, 'farming has … been described as a step backwards for human health'. He lists the advantages of the hunter-gatherer or foraging life: continual exercise ('tough on the elderly or disabled'); a low-fat diet; less tedium than with the farmer's repetitive 'grinding toil'; not having your doings piling up around you for the endless flies (medieval houses excavated in York show dogs' turds and rotting middens hard by the kitchens); no crowding; better teeth and fewer dropping out. But great inventions seem to have a habit of turning sour, from writing (Homer to *Hello!*), to the internal combustion engine. You can't undo inventions. Once slipped from the leash, they are free to proliferate, mutate, do good or bad or both at once. The stunning shift from killer thigh-bone in the hands of a hominid to a nuclear-powered space station in Kubrick's *2001: A Space Odyssey* famously said it all.

Hunting-and-gathering appears ecologically sound, which is why it gets such a good press these days. Recent research suggests otherwise. In eventually becoming the world's most successful predator, our species doomed whole swathes of mega-fauna. A brain wired for innovation and a unique combination of physical characteristics – tireless long legs, a twistable waist, a flexible shoulder joint – meant that members of *Homo sapiens sapiens* could not only run for longer than any other animal but could extend their reach on a hurled, rather than a prodded, spear. Releasing the stored energy of a flexed bow in the form of a blade-tipped arrow meant an ever longer, more accurate reach with a truly deadly velocity. It may have taken countless generations to evolve, but this new technology was lethal to the great, lumbering animals that hominids had only pranced around or scavenged for millions of years previously.

The mammoth in the room is the population question: such an existence kept planetary numbers to a manageable proportion, or even the plant-gathering alone might have exhausted the environment as alarmingly as our own bullying, target-driven ways are exhausting it. There is no proof that prehistoric peoples cared less for their sick or old than we do, generally speaking; it's just that the medical barriers between raw nature's claws and the human body amounted to some herbal concoctions and a lot of pleading to the gods. Sustainability, however precarious (the doomed megafauna aside), was possible only because our numbers were kept down.

Emphases change, however: in *Our Early Ancestors*, published as a basic introduction in 1926, the Cambridge archaeologist M.C. Burkitt stresses the precarities of the hunting life only to admit that farming was not all good: it brought 'the modern world and all its problems' – the biggest for Burkitt being war, not surprisingly. Later, discussing the modernity of the Sumerian Bronze Age, he jokes that nevertheless 'unemployment was less rife!' We see everything from our particular hill in time.

From our own Western twenty-first-century hill of computer screens, mobile phones, obesity and robot leaf-blowers, I would stress the communal sense of purpose that both the Mesolithic and the Neolithic peoples must have felt: the shared skills, the use of their hands, their fingers nimble and their sinews taut. The exchange of ideas, new thoughts, fresh approaches, yes... but always this sense of purpose granted by acquired, generational skills all but bred in the bone. Most folk dead before they got useless, but all time is relative: perhaps thirty-odd years of that kind of life was time enough. Perhaps facing each day and all its natural challenges with nothing but a natural toolkit and stitched-skin clothes gives the hours a quite different stretch. Full satisfaction guaranteed, lots of fresh air, who needs pain and age?

But pain they had: torn-off kneecaps, bad teeth, the lot.

And there's another thing that prevents one being flooded by warm, primitivist nostalgia: one great divide that leaves this whole question of life quality up in the air and unresolved.

Gender.

We have no idea how women were treated in prehistory, other than the likelihood of them being tasked with the nut- and fruit-gathering: possibly not treated very well by our standards, but the emphasis on fertility (even before farming) is telling. Women give birth, men don't. It hardly needs to be said that fertility involves a better deal for the man. When my wife was pregnant with our first child, we joined the Natural Childbirth Trust and Michel Odent, the famous underwater-delivery guru, gave a stirring lecture during which he showed us films of African village women giving birth: out of doors, squatting, alone – the woman barely showing pain, taking the slithery, blood-smeared infant into her arms and suckling it, the umbilical cord not immediately cut.

Was this how it was in ancient Britain, if all went well? Or was this merely being selective, just home-birth propaganda? And as for motherhood itself... should the mother have survived problems like postpartum haemorrhage (currently at an incidence rate of 27.5 per cent in Africa), how did the mothers (or fathers, for that matter) cope with loss, since prehistoric infant mortality has been calculated at 50 per cent? By avoiding too much attachment? But can mothers, once the hormones kick in after the delivery, counter their instinct to cherish, to love? A feminist reading of prehistory led the curators of the recent Ice Age Art exhibition at the British Museum to suggest that the little bone sculptures of female figurines with massive breasts and thighs and swollen bellies were carved by women: pure speculation, but at least it jarred the viewer out of any sexist assumptions that these early Michelangelos were male.

As an unreconstructed teenager in the 1970s, I would imagine being a bloke back in those pre-farming days, pacing softly out of a forest with my body charged and limber, the limp deer over my shoulders, heading back to my woman and my soup, my face woaded, tough as old boots at twenty-three, chock-full of intricate knowledge about plants and animals, about the way trees move in wind and the clouds scud, the way the moon unnerves behind fast-racing clouds and prompts our protective charms and prayers, because our charms are the best… and my woman running out to greet me with her lovely ripe smell of unwashed flesh, all chestnuts and beech-mast and smoke.

Or, to quote Walt Whitman: 'The scent of these armpits is aroma finer than prayer.'

I would feel that this technological nightmare I had been born into was a temporary blip. Short of an abscess or an axe in the skull, exile was the worst that could happen to you in the Neolithic, a living death; and sometimes I'd feel in exile from my own time. It was as if I had never had time to adjust, in evolutionary terms. It was as if my brain had got used to stuff over two million years, and then it had all changed too quickly, so that I was at sea. I'd walk between the great prairie fields up on the chalk hills and see the fluttering empty plastic sacks of chemical fertiliser, or duck my head as a tractor-borne spray-boom brought that toxic tang of pesticides on the downland wind, and feel bewildered by the present. I'd lie awake in the dorm that gave directly onto the Bath Road's lead-filled exhaust fumes, or stir sleeplessly in my various digs later, and wonder what on earth that swish and roar was all about. Cars and lorries? Too recent, too new. I felt at home in Africa, in more ways than one. But then, let's face it, I wasn't living in a bush village.

When I try to imagine what it was like to live on such an empty island, I think of a present-day village in the highlands of Nepal. A tiny settlement smoking from its fires, the barking of dogs, the laughter of children, the calls of herders, all of it surrounded by an epic landscape that stretches seemingly forever.

It doesn't matter that the landscapes bear no resemblance: it's the feel.

Night after night in the dorm I'd use my torch under the covers and read, not *Penthouse*, but my favourite book, a soft-cover book about Bruegel with big colour plates, and disappear into the paintings of crowded medieval villages, of workers in sixteenth-century harvest fields, of skating and feasting and dancing and hunting. I know, it sounds weird, but that's how it was. At university I was to transfer all this time-slipped feeling into a passion for Amerindians – the Apache, the Sioux, the wisdom of the Hopi. It wasn't just the hippy thing, but I guess it wasn't unfashionable either. A cynic would label it Romantic, capital R. Visiting past lives under hypnosis merely stirred the mix thicker: walking through eighteenth-century London as a rogue called Ralph Baker, I used period slang and had to research the meanings afterwards. Sometimes I felt I was a walking hybrid of past and present. Since these sessions were conducted in my student room in the early hours of the morning, I began to head inexorably towards a koala-eyed breakdown.

When in 1979 I finally visited a Hopi village out on its mesa in Arizona, preparations were underway in the underground kiva for the Butterfly Dance. We were the only whites. I was overcome at one point by nausea and dizziness. 'Strong energies,' said my companion. A Hopi woman invited us in to her adobe house near the temple: on her mantelpiece was a picture of her son in US Army uniform, next to a Bang and Olufsen stereo.

I knew that the great ladder emerging from the kiva symbolises the emergence of the initiate into the world of light and knowledge and of humility, a humility encouraged by a deep knowledge of the laws of nature, and sensed the arrogance of white America ringing the horizon. I guess that deep knowledge could be equivalent to our science, but our science is amoral and objective, or it wouldn't be science. What the Hopi know is that nature has to be respected, and that we are linked to it by our innermost subjectivity, our souls. That everything is connected. That nature will always try to redress imbalance. If only science could be hitched to wisdom instead of pure knowledge. If only it could put compassion and the sanctity of life first.

The extraordinary complexity of the Hopi way has always made me wonder about prehistoric beliefs. About how much we have lost beyond the bones and pottery and monoliths.

What about the bullies of the Mesolithic and the Neolithic? The ones that showed their teeth, firmly of the chimpanzee strain rather than the gentler bonobo? What kind of set-up did prehistoric people live under? Did their leaders demand stories – stories or else? Were the bullies in charge, or the wise, clear-sighted priestly ones? Was kindliness a prerequisite of being a clan chief, or muscle and brawn and ruthlessness? A big voice, or big brains? Were those with manipulative personality disorder in charge even then? Did the people cower under Gadaffi-like maniacs, utterly vulnerable to their every whim, or did some organic decency mean that the psychopaths were dealt with early on, before they tipped the fragile balance of survival into catastrophe? Hens, apparently, avoid nasty or aggressive or devious cocks, thus natural selection keeps the latter to a minimum. But such cocks can still thrive in human communities. Was Silbury the product of a crazed slave-driving tyrant, the lunatic vision of a Neolithic Kim Jong-il and his progeny? Perhaps things were more complicated: when the last king of Sri Lanka, Sri Vikrama Rajasinha, decided to use forced labour to build Kandy Lake in 1807, and a hundred of his counsellors advised against it, he had them all impaled in the bed of the future lake; yet he is regarded as a weak man surrounded by conspirators rather than a mad ogre.

Alternatively, Silbury might have been a brilliant means to unite a people with a common project that gave their brief lives a meaning

In other words, were the builders of Silbury more like the Hopi, or did they tend (even slightly) to the Aztec – a famously deranged culture where a father could sell his daughter as a sexual slave or a religious sacrifice for a few hundred cacao beans, and where a peaceful death in bed was feared most of all as the portal to unbearable tortures in the after-life, and where the sun only turned in the sky if you satisfied its omnivorous appetite for human blood and just about anything else that could be consumed? (This last a synonym for the free-market economy, perhaps.)

If recorded history is anything to go by, or anthropologists' reports of preliterate communities to be trusted, then communities would have shown the full gamut of possibilities, even when they were believing in roughly the same thing. When our theatre company was touring the downland villages, I was struck by how varied they were – from welcoming and relaxed to stiff and snooty: it depended on a matrix of factors – social divisions, community history, power structures, the immediate geography and so on. Equally I was assured, when in Cameroon, that 'pagan' villages could vary wildly in their type of worship: traditional African belief could result in a happy, tolerant and pleasant place to live, or somewhere full of fear and even terror. (There was also, of course, variation in the overtly Christian or Muslim villages.) So the witchdoctor who treated our tall houseboy Joseph's sick little daughter and overcharged him and prescribed rolling her each day in the mud of a crocodile-infested river and gave the father some herbal highs that sent his eyes red and drove him to appear in our living room one day wielding a kitchen knife and shouting crazy stuff, was probably a bad man, a fraud, an extortionist – but that didn't make all witchdoctors bad, nor the belief system itself. Oil and coal are not catastrophic in themselves; they have been made catastrophic by their uncontrolled exploiters (and their acquiescent users); by the devil's pact our society has made with comfort, convenience and profit.

Perhaps around Silbury it depended on who was in charge, or on the history of the tribe, or on what traumas had visited them, or the psychological make-up of the high priest, shaman, witchdoctor, what-have-you. Some of these may have been Rasputins, others Gandalfs. Maybe, during the construction of Silbury Hill, Gandalfs were replaced by Rasputins, and then by someone wishy-washy and his wishier-washier nephew, and then it all ran out of steam and grass grew long upon the flanks, and then it all started again under a messianic woman with a vision and the full size we have now was reached in record time – thirty years, say, by which time vision woman was in her fifties with a face like a wizened apple and no teeth, keeping permanently in her hut where the leaders could visit her for advice, each wondering when the people could stop humping baskets of chalk up and lay down their picks and ox shoulder blades and call it a day, because it was already bigger than anything they had ever seen, and blazing white, and the ditch had several feet of water in it, and the people were not like their parents, they had lost the buzz, they had to be whipped every so often (or worse) *pour encourager les autres*.

And the vision woman probably said: 'I wish to meet my ancestors.' And she climbed the gigantic mound. And the effort, as she blinked in the unfamiliar light, stumbling and straining without a helping shoulder, the people gaping from below, did actually kill her upon the summit, except that it took a day and a night of lying up there on the fresh chalk that was cold as mashed bones, staring into the sun and into the moon, before the ancestors came for her.

The hardest to imagine, perhaps, is the lack of people: Burl demolished a colleague's theory that Avebury's sloping banks might have accommodated 48,000 people by pointing out that 'such a number of people might have comprised the entire population of western Europe.' The fifteen square miles of the Avebury 'complex' could not have supported more than 500 mouths; when the earliest farmers settled here some thousand or so years before, bringing their cattle, they might have been no more than three or four families, pioneers tramping in from wherever had grown too crowded, too disputed. Before their arrival, the forests and scrubbier uplands would have seen only the occasional hunting-and-gathering band, camping for a while until they moved on, ever restless, with no conception of the soil actually belonging to someone.

Why did they ever move on, given that moving home is a pain? Possibly because they would follow migrating herds, or – as mentioned earlier – exhaust local resources. The Neanderthal technique of mass killings of the larger mammals by driving them over cliffs, if this is what the Neanderthal hunters did (it is a controversial interpretation of the evidence), had perhaps already begun to bite into sustainability when restless modern humans adopted it; why otherwise take up farming as a good idea?

The older good idea certainly lasted. The earliest group of hunters in Britain (belonging to a hominid species several stages before *Homo sapiens*) has been dated to either 840,000 or 950,000 years BC, based on microliths and fossilised footprints of family groups found on the Norfolk coast. The northern climate was cooling, that we know, and Britain heading towards another of its Arctic periods, yet these people – possibly unclothed and without fire – survived despite few edible plants: summers were chilly, winters would have gone below zero.

Adaptation meant that they might not have felt cold as we do. Hunting-and-gathering has a long tradition, yes, but the time span is impossible to grasp: it is mere numbers. We are impressed by the archaeologists' dating powers, yet their indecision in this case spells a difference of 100,000 years – a length of time that, unwound from now, returns us to the Palaeolithic, long before *Homo sapiens sapiens* left Africa.

Like Silbury herself, time changes size depending on how you look at it and where you look at it from. For want of time, we never get enough done. Yet I doubt the builders of Silbury thought like this: there might never have been a want of the stuff, because it was a continual roll unnotched by clocks, on which the past was visible not as something recorded (old photos, old manuscripts) but as something that hung around, part of the same material as the present, a touch ghostly but just as potent as living flesh.

Each stage of the mound – with its several smaller versions within – is a concrete incorporation of time, the eternal 'now' lying within the living moment of which it is part. There is no such thing as the past. The hill lives and the generations live within it. Earth – the element we walk on and dig out and heap up with our antler picks, our baskets – is the embodiment of the movement of time: renewing itself each spring, cyclical, not linear. Of course the prehistoric mind never put it like this, but this is what it might have understood: a great, saving wisdom, in which death is manageable. Otherwise to be conscious of mortality is unbearable, an unbearable thing.

Time in the conventional sense did not really exist. Where I live in France, in the Cévennes mountains, farming families would plant an oak sapling to ensure that future generations might have a fine straight roof-beam for the inevitable extension. Their great-grandchildren were just as much of the now. The practice has stopped. Time's tyranny has resumed. When Edward Thomas, whose love for the Downs kept him sane, saw a farmer by his beech-shrouded thatched barn along the Pilgrim's Way, 'a thick, bent, knotty man', he reflected how 'life is a dark simple matter for him; three-quarters of his living is done for him by the dead; merely to look at him is to see a man five generations thick, so to speak…' That was over a century ago, before intensive farming turned the countryside into a managerial balance sheet and tomorrow was what mattered.

We moderns bounce about on a great column of time, ever growing, its roots countless generations below. Our conceptions are rational, scientific, full of measurements and the gunk that society fills us with, along with old superstitions and atavistic fears and moments of profundity and beauty. We have no idea of how to live within nature's means: each generation has its own desires, its own needs, always more or less excessive. Listen to the A4 as it clips the side of Silbury, or at least the ditch: the rush of it, the pain of the noise, the stupidity.

Wordsworth saw it all coming, of course.

> The world is too much with us: late and soon,
> Getting and spending, we lay waste our powers;
> Little we see in Nature that is ours:
> We have given our hearts away, a sordid boon!

At night, the A4 becomes from afar a twinkling sequence of fairy lights moving slowly, red and white, like an obscure code that shows the machine is operative, that reducing society's principal motives to the dry imperatives of the market, to the impossible goal of limitless wealth, a wealth created by whatever rings the till, good or bad (arms, tropical hardwoods, dodgy pharmaceuticals, whatever), is still functional. That we have other gods, and they will be appeased and obeyed.

Did we ever have it right? Bronze Age farmers cleared the forests yard by yard, a colossal labour that has left us the bare-limbed downs stretching high and clean and dry above the tangled, moist, gravelly lowlands beyond. The ruralist H.J. Massingham, who liked to dress in Neolithic robes and called modern society 'an utter darkness and savagery', wrote beautifully of the downs he loved for that muscular bareness and confused it with the purity of the primordial, admiring Wiltshire especially for 'the true, the aboriginal upper chalk [that] emerges in its natural soil and purest outlines... Here are no prodigal woods nor shady coverts, since only the juniper and, more doubtfully, the yew, are the legitimate children of the chalk.'

This is rubbish, of course: all except the most windswept patches of the downs were originally covered in trees, the wildwood diminishing dramatically only from the second millennium BC, with the increase of sheep. The bleak purity was an offshoot of the swung axe, just as New York's scintillant beauty is an offshoot of competitive, pragmatic capitalism. 'Avebury and its barrows,' he writes, 'reflect the monumental simplicity of Wiltshire, as Stonehenge and its barrows reflect its smooth round surfaces.' One of Avebury's barrows, of course, is 'the towering pyramid of Silbury'. Massingham, believing bareness to be the downs' birthright, sees her as eminently at home. Her sheer oddity is rendered invisible in the blaze of his personal vision, passionately in love with the idea of the primordial, the unchanged nature of the chalk hills.

In my own 1930s copy of *English Downland* there is a photo of Silbury with some foreground sheep nibbling tussocks in a pen of wattled hurdles that is enclosed, in turn, by an example of what Massingham thought of as 'shameful': barbed wire strung between concrete posts. It took great skill to make a gently curved hurdle out of green hazel rods, and it was a specialist trade: most downland villages had their own hurdle-maker. So here in a nutshell – or rather, in an English field – we have an accidental palimpsest of ancient, historical and modern. It is likely that hurdles were prehistorical, in fact: it is the kind of element that does not survive, one of the myriad absences that distorts our vision of the unrecorded past.

We are all Massinghams, of course: our passions distort, and even the most cautious, scrupulously scientific, strictly data-based approach is a distortion, since almost nothing is left of the vivid, messy truth that is life as actually lived. Nothing of the poetry.

The more accurate version of primordial downland has its own poetry. In Avebury's museum, there is a screen on which a realistic bird's-eye view of the area changes millennia at the touch of a button: the first image is a matted density of forest with the odd upland knuckle showing clean. Imagine such a thing. A forest teeming with wild animals, deadly and lovely, uncut underbrush and gleeful ivy and liana ropes of climbers like wild honeysuckle – as thick and buzzy with insects as the forests of Cameroon or the swamps of Louisiana. Rustles and thuds of brown bears, wild boars, lumbering aurochs, running packs of wolves. A yew bow and a few flint arrowheads between you and a merciless predator... which could be man. From another hunter clan. Eyes flickering, the pace agile and quiet as he follows you. The rain and the cold: only a little warmer than today.

Then the screen shifts to 2500 BC and the clearings begin, a thread-like track for the A4, the oval openness of the vast causewayed enclosure of Windmill Hill... The surgical cuts for Silbury and Avebury and the Sanctuary, the connecting avenues, in what has become a patchwork of grass and juniper scrub and the odd brown tilth among the furry trees. And so on, until the furriness has almost all gone, surviving only east of Marlborough in the ancient, royal collar of Savernake Forest, or in tiny tufts of copses and spinneys and beech hangars.

That is what man does. Masters, decides, acts. Propitiates, in the old days. Now we no longer bother. Now simple propitiation isn't enough.

Six

It was the scratch-farmers, the herders, who built the tombs, the long barrows of stone tamped over with turf. Pure nomads don't bother with such things, such markers of territorial rights, letting earth be fathomed by the dead. Hunter-gatherers move on, dictated to by circumstance, supply and demand, floods and fires, or perhaps what the shaman tells them, if shamans they have.

Fleet and light on their feet, with better teeth unscored by grit and husk, a more natural and varied diet of wild gleanings than the same old same old of crops, perhaps they were at least easier in their skin, with – let me repeat it – an ancient human ancestry in our islands alone of around 900,000 years, interspersed by some fifteen periods of glaciation when ice up to three miles thick scoured everything to bedrock. The last Ice Age was recent, 12,000 years back, covering most of Scotland, Wales, Ireland and the north of England: we are in what is called an interglacial period. Statistically, the climatic norm at this latitude is ice and freezing winds. We are temporarily reprieved by mildness.

Glaciation provided some of the dullest of my geography lessons: terminal moraine just about summed it up. Our brains were too green to take it all in, perhaps: even now

I find it forbidding, but more because geology requires a compartmentalising of the mind or it would freeze any sentient being with horror. We were told that the downs were once shallow seas, the white levels of chalk created from billions of shells of marine invertebrates, minuscule balls of algae falling slowly through the water over millions of years and piling up like boredom. In all this time, no being capable of self-consciousness looked upon it. There was ravening and there was quiet feeding. Birth and death. Comfort and pain. But no one knew in the way a human knows.

I wasn't particularly exercised by this consciousness of immense stretches of pointlessness, as youth gave me a sense that I was here for a purpose, newly landed and special, with ages still to go, if not outright immortality. The brain survives by careful selection of the truths that reality displays: watching the grass sway and ripple on a cornfield had always – ever since I had noticed it from the games pitch of my previous school – moved me in a way I found intensely pleasurable. So much so that it interfered with my ability to follow the ball, whatever the sport, because the sport in question suddenly seemed silly, the game shallow.

Depths were revealing themselves and I was a willing receptor. I was, I suppose, a child of Wordsworth, not so keen on 'getting and spending'. I felt an affinity with landscape, did not like the urban. I had a very clear idea of the country-and-city divide. After all, much of my boyhood was spent in Chesham, in the beech-covered Chilterns, on the very end of the Metropolitan Line (we kept a maisonette there while in Cameroon). Now and again I would go up to London in one of the Met Line's unpainted aluminium stock – silvery like a UFO – staring at the ribbed wooden floor crammed with cigarette stubs; we'd hum along feeling very modern, and pass thickening brick suburbia until the clashing, brash and self-important heart of the capital embraced us.

Rather naively, I felt sorry for children who lived there. My mother, a (half-Scottish) Londoner herself, loved it, as did my grandmother, who had escaped poverty in Sheffield by becoming a teacher in 1918. They had both lived through the Blitz, which might have deepened their affection. My father, brought up in rural Derbyshire, did not like it. The muddy bomb sites were being replaced by huge structures of white concrete and glass with cavernous, ambiguous entrances, but the stone and brick were still grimy, the buses spewing out sooty diesel, the adults in hats with umbrellas and handbags hurrying down gulfs of streets that seemed to my short legs to go on and on past the chrome bumpers and high-up yellow signs demanding *Player's Please*.

I lived in London for seven years during the 1980s and now, visiting several times a year, I appreciate the sprawl for its own singular depths, its endless shifting layers, the finding of what in Iain Sinclair's psychogeographical terms has not been erased so much as 'reforgotten'. (Fittingly, Sinclair made a silent film in 1972 – an 'alchemical fable' called *Maggot Street* – which ends with a pilgrimage from Whitechapel to Silbury Hill.) Archaeology deals in literal depths, while poetry deals with metaphorical depths. For a time I confused the two. I still do, I suppose. It doesn't help that prehistoric measurements appear to be based on the fathom, from the Old English word for a pair of outstretched arms: about 6 feet, or 2 yards, from fingertip to fingertip. Fathoms are often used in discussions of, say, Avebury and Stonehenge: in an age before tape measures, a man used the dimensions of his own body as well as the stuff around him. It's guesswork when applied to preliterate societies, but it makes sense and the field evidence fits. From a 'poppyseed' (a quarter of a barleycorn), through a 'shaftment' (width of the hand and outstretched thumb) or a 'cubit' (fingertips to elbow) to a 'fathom', we are in the real and sensual and human world. I can visualise them, estimate them. Metrical units are pure and soulless mathematics. If our modern world is ruled by anything, it is the latter.

I especially like the mixture of surface and depth implied in the fathom: a body had always to be buried a fathom deep, the height of a tallish person. As my Shakespeare-addicted grandmother used to intone:

> Full fathom five thy father lies;
> Of his bones are coral made;
> Those are pearls that were his eyes:
> Nothing of him that doth fade
> But doth suffer a sea-change
> Into something rich and strange.

Silbury Hill's purpose is unfathomable, although I have seen it claimed that measuring her base produces an intended diameter of 100 fathoms; this requires a fathom to be 5½ feet, and 100 sounds suspiciously decimal. Professor Alexander Thom, who held the chair of engineering science at Brasenose College, Oxford, briefly reconciled high maths and ancient monuments, claiming to have found an accurate prehistoric unit of measurement, the Megalithic yard, not based on pacing out but on geometrical calculation. His ideas, to which he devoted much of his life, have since been debunked, but I remember them being the subject of much excitement in the oft-cranky 1970s: the stone circles became astronomical observatories that had served a people who were astonishingly good at geometry and long-term calendrical prediction.

Much can be conjured from purely natural phenomena. If you stand patiently in a field to the east of Silbury, where aerial photographs of crop marks revealed the unsighted ghosts of two huge palisaded enclosures straddling the Kennet (consisting of over 4,000 lofty oak posts rising from oval ditches), you will notice how the setting sun 'rolls' up or down Silbury's slope on certain days in the year (especially in early May); on these days the slope corresponds to the angle of the sun's path. Neither too steep, nor too shallow. It is viewable on YouTube and is beautiful, even haunting. But it is hard to imagine that our Neolithic ancestors would have gone to so much trouble for such a frail interaction with whatever entity they thought the sun was. It is possible that they never actually noticed it happening, even when the hill was complete; on the other hand, calendars using the horizon with all its notches and bumps silhouetted against the sun, moon and stars are known to have existed among, say, the ancestral Pueblos in America's Southwest, having gelled into practice from generations of quiet observation. Altering that horizon to build something as large as Silbury has no historical precedent, and again would have required mathematical powers of prediction.

Thom has his disciples, including archaeoastronomer Nicholas Mann, who has spent equal decades exploring what he believes to be the Neolithic people's highly advanced cosmological knowledge: in *Avebury Cosmos* he revives the night sky, packed with southern stars (based on the 26,000-year rotation of the Earth's axis) as it would have appeared back then, and is convinced that Avebury and Silbury were intimately related to this awe-inspiring vision of the entire Milky Way. It is all very seductive, but the kind of archaeologists who get their knees muddy and eyes strained in the mess of digs tend to disapprove.

Back in the 1970s, I ploughed gamely through Keith Critchlow's *Time Stands Still*, one of the first to develop Thom's ideas. A large book with beautiful coloured photographs of Avebury and Stonehenge, it likewise posited a Neolithic genius for geometry a good two millennia before Plato: but I barely understood a word. I had expected some hard-nosed disclosure that would explicate my own feelings of some vague, simmering revelation round the corner – I was twenty-one, deep in that wobbly, hurtling transition period between childhood and adulthood, and the revelation was actually to do with growing up. The imminent truth was no more mysterious than the fact that I would mature and eventually die, but I pumped enough Celtic mist between me and it that I put it off, or at least gave it a more fascinating shape.

Am I being unfair to my younger self? He irritates me, because he seems so distracted, pulled away from living by dreaming. It is not surprising, since Silbury and Avebury and the Mound and the barrows were massive and mysterious dreams in the middle of a modern wakefulness, and that I experienced them while awake was not altogether easy. Have I made it clear that in my first two years at Marlborough, biking out into the downs, these dreams rather frightened me, if anything? I was desperate for normality, and none of these places offered it. Normality for me was not a brooding monolith or eerie hummock but a cosy beechwood or a meadow with horses in it or, to my slight embarrassment, the residential streets around town. There you could see into people's back gardens and glimpse their messy kitchens or sitting rooms; I'd walk there incessantly, supping on homely ordinariness.

My home then established itself over 3,000 miles away, and I couldn't contact it easily. The post took two weeks: now and again a rustly blue airmail letter with onion skin paper, the type that folded onto itself to make its own envelope, lay on the wooden bench in the corridor of my senior house – a surreal tessera from my other life. The address would be in my mother's handwriting, though the contents would always be typewritten. She typed faster than anyone I knew: secretarial training – essential for someone whose sight was going. I would take it off somewhere private (which usually meant up the local farm track) and sample it slowly: another fragment of domesticity, a tendril of root which an hour or so spent back in the school would effortlessly pluck out.

Eventually I tamped my apprehension of those ancient places and converted them into evocative ruins. I would bike up to West Kennet Long Barrow at dusk, its lengthy ridge-like profile black and vast-seeming against the deepening

sky. If nothing else, Wiltshire's ripening fields of barley were useful as coverts – lying down between the rows on a Saturday evening with schoolmates, I would escape the world on a potent mix of cider and beer, choking on a Player's No. 10. I read D.H. Lawrence's animal poems and wrote them out by hand. I discovered Eliot's *The Waste Land* – a modernist vegetation myth – in the school library, and so the first long poem of my own had careful notes: fortunately no one else set eyes on it. What I was discovering was the way words produced their own crystals of meaning, how poems grew and took shape partly of their own accord, the syllables attracting their own patterns through sound and association. An infinitely varied, part-magical formation that I had to learn to allow and not over-control. Something like Eliot's

> – Yet when we came back, late, from the hyacinth garden,
> Your arms full, and your hair wet, I could not
> Speak, and my eyes failed, I was neither
> Living nor dead, and I knew nothing,
> Looking into the heart of light, the silence.

My parents left Africa in my gap year; they found an affordable – plain and rather jerry-built – modern house in Berkshire (hardly the cottage I had dreamed of), in a hamlet five miles north of Newbury, on the edge of the downland. I knew Wiltshire, but not Berkshire. I fell for the downs all over again, because the Berkshire portion – opening out in the west of the county – is subtly different. (I have always ignored the Tories' ludicrous county boundary changes of 1974, which neglected 1,000 years of tradition as well as geology and passed those chalk downs to gravel-and-clay Oxfordshire, turning oval Berkshire into a sausage.)

Massingham clearly prefers Berkshire's chalklands to Wiltshire's, convinced that these 'genuinely unknown' downs 'establish their own identity'. The lack of river valleys, the 'gentler slopes and smoother gradients' create subtler modulations, enhanced by an extraordinary lack of villages in Berkshire's heart, where I would walk as much as I could – loving especially the broad open magnificence of the barrow-dotted valley between Lambourn and, to the north, the great chambered tomb of Wayland's Smithy abutting the Ridgeway.

There was something about the brackeny, umber-and-cream colouring of that downland, a certain sea-breeze

dryness to the air, that distinguished it from the area to the west – which was otherwise identical in geological terms. The glorious emptiness was also due to the way the few villages on the map managed to hide themselves – 'sequestered', as Massingham puts it, 'partly by trees and partly by trivial dips in the ground.' The Oxford road, the A34, cut through it to the east with the usual brutality, and the M4 motorway

pounded through to the south: we lived just below the latter, so close it was audible as a somnolent drone.

This horror somehow set off the beech woods and small

oak-dotted fields and tumbledown labourer's cottage with its little pond that lay just a steep muddy path away above my parents' house, secret places that were made doubly poignant therefore by looking out on a monstrous pullulating scar, and nourishing my anti-technological paranoia (the fact that the motorway allowed my father to commute each day to Heathrow was discreetly ignored). The small fields have now gone, the great white dazzle of a quarry lapping right up to the outer beech trunks: once a landscape's been vandalised, you might as well wreck it completely. Vacancy. All I have left are some chalk-pastel sketches: hedges, a line of oak trees, that tumbledown cottage and its tangled pond – the sketches dating from my brief desire to be a painter.

I'm expressing much of this in the past tense: I haven't been back there for years, and my parents are long dead. My first novel, *Ulverton* – the name of an imaginary village in the Berkshire uplands – was set close to the border with Wiltshire, and it was mostly written in France. But it was given to me by the downland earth: the whole idea of recounting a village over hundreds of years, but with stories connected solely by place and rumour and garbled memory, not genealogy, came to me whole on a February walk in crisp sunlight.

I was already living in London, and was on a weekend family visit. Pausing by a wooden gate set in a broad old hedge full of wild clematis, I wondered what lost stories this ancient opening had been witness to, and how to express that loss in a novel, and ideas began to accrete. In the context of the English countryside, at least, loss seemed to have the edge on continuity. A little later, musing on the idea as I crossed a flint-strewn field near a farm where I used to work in the holidays – stacking hay bales, building a rick, doing odd jobs like mending fences – I suddenly felt an electric charge coming up through the earth and into my legs.

This is good, said the soil. This is the land speaking, and all its dead. Go for it.

Perhaps this is what the people felt in the vicinity of the stone circles or on and around the giant mounds: an electric charge, as if suddenly earthed and in contact. This is the land speaking, and all its dead. Go for it.

This was a long time after my university stretch, during which my equilibrium wobbled: those were heady, vatic days – with a good dose of crankiness. As the world around me appeared to be either wading gratefully through rising levels of consumer delights or bellowing hard-left slogans with a boorish intolerance, I sought the sacred – along with many others on the edge of the counter-culture. This was the 1970s: can you blame us? Finding the sacred was hard work, in more ways than one. I didn't want it to rest wishy-washy, I wanted it to be imprinted and concrete, and that aforementioned numerological aspect persuaded me because I was virtually innumerate.

It would have been more sensible to have stayed with the downs, for all that their delicate beauty was being tested by the claw hammer of Euro-agribusiness, a mad state of affairs that was obsessing me more and more. I should have stayed with the inscape of observable things – with the peewits that shrieked over us as we built the high rick, or the sunken lane on which I saw a hare in perfect profile, stopped dead a few yards away, or with the secret paths between tangles of traveller's joy: paths that I felt no one had seen since the world went neo-fascist Henry Ford instead of neo-socialist William Morris. I'd have done much better to have found enough solace in the landscape; to have followed the example of Edward Thomas, who set out walking and walking and found plenty of miracles in the woods and the fields, in 'the elephantine downs going west in the rain... where I see and touch with the eye and enjoy the shapes of each bole and branch in turn.'

To 'see feelingly', as the blind Gloucester has it in *King Lear*. The sensory, immediate world. But I was lured away by mystery and abstraction. By the deep past. Mystery allows us space to breed our own fantasies: an airliner crashing into the ocean is merely tragic; an airliner vanishing into thin air is tragic but fascinating. If Silbury was suddenly to be decoded, her original purpose established for certain thanks to some new discovery, would she be so beautiful and alluring? Might she even become a straightforward 'it'? Would the countless blogs and commentaries clustering around her — far outnumbering academic papers — start to thin?

Attempts to decode her through numbers were legion some thirty years ago. The accepted theory now is that geometric figures are malleable — it did occur to me that accurate measurement in a tussocky field of monoliths with irregular stone surfaces, let alone of a massive, rough-hewn chalk hill, was a challenge. The present consensus is that prehistoric peoples stretched their arms out and paced and spread their fingers wide and were not too concerned about accuracy: not that they were jobsworths, it was just that certain concepts had not yet materialised as theory. Strict accuracy was nowhere visible in nature, which must have made the human efforts like Silbury Hill or Stonehenge seem even more remarkable in a symmetrical and geometrical way (anachronistic terms though these are) than they do to us. The lines and patterns scratched on ancient pottery are often beautifully complex,

but they are variable and wonky and rough and full of life, as most lines are in the natural world (except where something is breaking along a fracture line, perhaps, such as stamped-on ice). That maths lies under everything in the universe is neither here nor there: in the prehistoric world, what lay under everything was the ischium – the pelvic bone on which the body rests when sitting – belonging to the Great Goddess. Or whatever. We just don't know.

Alexander Thom, originally in aeronautics, poured himself into the mystery, the enigma: the Megalithic became a branch of the engineering department. We all did that: converting the past into something that spoke to us, even when we thought it was utterly other. Was it so other? Perhaps these extraordinary monuments were no more than massive efforts by thinking, reasoning people to build something well-crafted, striking and unnatural. To dominate the landscape, whether as an expression of temporal power against a human competitor, or through a spiritual impulse. There is continuity in that expression and that impulse: the World Trade Centre, Chartres cathedral. Sometimes both at the same time.

Yet if it all seemed hopelessly beyond our calculations, we turned the dial even further and called on UFOs, aliens that were really our shadow-selves. We still do it. A quick search on the internet proves it. Projection is various in its effects, from benign to deeply damaging, but it is a product of being human. Silbury or Avebury or Stonehenge and their like are great blank screens.

That's not quite right: that in itself is an exaggeration. Bits of the picture are tantalisingly visible, peeled into view by archaeologists. Stonehenge is currently where it's all at. I've always felt a bit snooty about Stonehenge: its awful car park and toilets, its ghastly green pedestrian ribbon, its Watford-like underpass, its international celebrity status, its summer solstice shenanigans. When I first visited one afternoon as a boy, you could walk among the stones, stroke them, climb on the fallen giants, pose for a snapshot with no one behind.

My second visit a few years later was a shock: I vowed never to return. It felt as if no one quite knew what to do with Stonehenge, like an elderly, slightly embarrassing relative. Roads were built and houses constructed in the name of progress and all that seemed to matter was getting the tourists in and out. The rock festivals helped not a bit: the stones were just a kind of Spinal Tap décor, beleaguered and faintly ridiculous (Spinal Tap's spoof song 'Stonehenge' – 'Nobody knows who they were, or what they were doing' – caught the mood brilliantly and is still wincingly funny to watch.)

So I have tended to see Stonehenge as the Tesco to

Avebury's Waitrose. English Heritage's multi-million revamp – a tactfully distant visitor's centre, the adjacent main road closed and grassed over – can't dampen the sickly night-time glow from the neon-lit business park and Holiday Inn just two miles away, and the necessity of a shuttle bus service seems questionable: what's wrong with legs or, for the sick or disabled, wheelchairs? No, my absurd snobbery has not been swept aside by this long overdue make-over but by recent revelations from the trowel. Since the last century's excavation results were brought out of obscurity and published in 1995, Stonehenge's aura has been pumped with new vigour. The collective spirit that built it (who could have coerced so many?) is reflected in the Riverside Project, consisting of over a hundred shovellers led by Mike Parker Pearson of the University of Sheffield: their latest discoveries are remarkable, blowing away some of the mystic mist yet making of the monument something even more arresting and vivid.

They first uncovered more of a vast settlement of small, square wattle-and-daub huts at nearby Durrington Walls, a massive henge enclosure with traces of two impressive timber circles within its banks. Working on a hunch, the team revealed a paved road from the henge down to the River Avon. The village likely served the thousands of builders needed to construct the stone circle, although a similar settlement discovered near the Pyramid of Cheops is now thought to have been a military quarters: the Egyptian workers probably made do with tents in the quarries.

The Durrington Walls huts may also have served the seasonal pilgrims who came for the ensuing ceremonies. Numerous remains of animal bones suggest that, at every winter solstice, thousands of people travelled to Salisbury Plain from as far away as the Orkneys (nearly 800 miles) and met up for the mammoth ancestor of our Christmas lunch. Parker Pearson is convinced that the builders and the pilgrims were one and the same, that these people were there to work as well as feast: Stonehenge was, in other words, a collective 'megaconstruction' that brought unity to the island. Its stony temenos was echoed in wood by the tall timber circles two miles away, while Woodhenge, just outside the Durrington henge, was possibly a large-scale prototype of the later monument in sarsen and bluestone – balsa-wood to the concrete, as it were.

I have problems imagining a journey of 800 miles through myriad tribal territories, but this may be because any contemporary vision of island unity and peacefulness has been corroded by recorded history. Perhaps the pilgrims wore amulets or feathers to signify their status, or were smeared in ash and naked like Indian sadhus (the climate was slightly milder), or face-painted in bright pigments with their hair coiled in great knots above their forehead – left to complete their one holy pilgrimage by the locals' fear of divine reprisal. Or perhaps there was indeed loss of life on the muddy, wintry route: the danger was part of the sacredness, as it was for Crusaders, as it is for those performing the Hajj.

The welcome closure of the A344 allowed the team to dig under the Stonehenge Avenue, which connects the circle to the River Avon a mile and a half away. They found it was built over an Ice Age landform consisting of two broad and parallel ridges with deep fissures in between; these had been clawed out by thawing meltwater after one of the more vehement periods of ancient glaciation. The ridges happen to be on the solstice axis; the team uncovered a ring of bluestones at the Avenue's far end, near the river. The discovery by another archaeologist of still-active warm springs at Vespasian's Camp just outside Amesbury, a short walk away, along with hearths and burnt aurochs bones dated to soon after the last Ice Age (some 12,000 years ago), suggests that the immediate area had long been known as a hunting ground on the aurochs migration route, and attracted people from a huge area.

It was, in other words, a place favoured by the ancestors: the circular pits in what was until recently the car park (they were marked in concrete) had already indicated massive posts dating from 8500 to 10000 BC, a time when there were no other monuments anywhere in the country and when at least the southern half of the island was spirited away under a dark fog of wildwood, but with open patches of grassland on the huge plain that made it unusual and, no doubt, attractive.

Parker Pearson, encouraged by numerous cremation burials found on the site – mostly of an apparent 'elite' – that predate the circle itself, believes that Stonehenge was a monument to the dead, a place of contact with the phantom ancestors (who had perhaps morphed into local, protective gods, much like Shinto *kami*). The henge at Durrington, on the other hand, was symbolic of life – suggested by the feasting and the fires and the close-packed huts.

More daringly, he conjectures a biannual processional journey between the two sites – down the paved avenue to the river (ancient symbol of life's journey) and along the riverbank, and then up that natural white track of ice-fissured rock towards the dazzling moment of the midsummer solstice sunrise or, in midwinter, the solstice sunset flooding the interior. After which darkling date, of course, the days grow longer. The sun dies but it needs reviving: with drums, a shouted charm, a gathering, a roar. A sacrifice, perhaps: although the three-year-old with his skull split, found near the centre of Woodhenge, is a rare example of ritual killing, this does not necessarily mean that the practice was rare at the time.

What happened when the thousands were shivering in freezing rain and you could barely distinguish the sun through the dismal gloom? Did the priests or shamans have something else up their voluminous sleeves? But then the glutinous Glastonbury Festival seems to survive its own climatological challenges. Maybe, as at Glastonbury, the important element was the gathering itself – probably equally well-oiled more than 4,000 years ago by alcohol (mead brewed from honey), along with so much food that these lean folk on their self-sufficient diet could not finish their plates: literally tons of food waste have been recovered, deliberately left as a material reminder.

While most feasting within henges was that of an elite, a statement of privilege and power – especially with the arrival of the Beaker culture – the glorious blow-out at Stonehenge was likely to have been for everyone who had made the trek, with whole pigs turned on their spits over the open fires. Plus (say the experts, supported by fragments of parallel evidence and some common-sense conclusions) a lot of free sex: fertility in the sapless season of death. Date, marriage, kids. Seed-time in midwinter.

She'll get to like Orkney, give her time. We've a fine herd.

However twenty-first century this all appears to be, it does seem that each year's discoveries support the narrative:

musing on the necessity of a gathering-place by the river, Parker Pearson finds one. The sacredness of rivers, their associations with the ancestors and death, is suggested by the lack of fish-bones in feasting or domestic waste: eating fish appears to have been taboo during the Neolithic. Birds, too: after all, they belong to the sky, where the gods reside.

Rival archaeologists such as Timothy Darvill find these latest theories 'simplistic', however, and prefer to see Stonehenge as a healing centre. That seduced me, too, when it was first mooted. Perhaps we're all just seeing what we want to see. I once saw an old man's bearded face in a wood's undergrowth and took a picture: and there he is, recorded. Evening light on bracken and bramble, if you study it carefully. I could be excused, but I might have built it up into an entire belief system.

What role did the Avebury complex play some twenty miles away? Was it the sacred place of a rival people, or tuned to the same wavelength?

No major excavation has been done there recently: the 2008 consolidation of Silbury revealed much about her construction, but nothing about her meaning. Unless, as we have seen Jim Leary propose, her meaning is her construction; the process of building was as important as any final result. But isn't that just a reflection of the current fashion for process? Process is all the rage in the art school where I teach, and where conceptual works are still favoured. Artists like Jackson Pollock or Sol LeWitt or Richard Long enact a secular version of the sacred ritual, where the end result is no more important than the journey to get there. Yet it seems vaguely anachronistic to apply such a vision to peoples whose overriding concerns were getting enough to eat and protecting their kith and kin from predators and enemies. Perhaps their belief – that the act of dumping gravel, turves and then endless basket loads of chalk rubble would protect them not just physically but spiritually – was so deep and powerful that it justified the effort. Human societies have done crazier things. The statues on Easter Island, for which experts think the entire island was denuded of trees, are a case in point. With Silbury Hill, however, a final stage was, in fact, reached – after which she stayed unchanged until at least the Saxon period.

Let us, nevertheless, make some cautious suppositions that have not yet been denied by the data.

The rings and hummocks were sacred spaces, ritualistic centres.

The people would gather in them or around them, many thousands travelling from very far away, at significant moments of the year – certainly at midwinter and possibly also at midsummer, at harvest-time.

The ceremonies were linked with fertility and death – both at once, rather than separately.

Avebury and Stonehenge were where the dead (possibly become protective gods) could be approached or honoured or appeased, thus ensuring their continuing help – if only by keeping away – with the harvest to come, or against raiders and invaders, or with the very turning of the sun.

Human sacrifice was involved at certain periods of use.

The way they were used was not stable, the meaning of these spaces changing over the generations, over the centuries; either process was more important than completion, or each stage felt significant and complete to its builders.

Paul Valéry said of a poem that it is 'never completed except by some accident such as weariness, satisfaction, the need to deliver, or death: for, in relation to who or what is making it, it can only be one stage in a series of inner transformations.' Perhaps these monuments too were poems of a kind, written into the landscape before writing came to northern Europe. But the impulse that drove people to dig up and drag sarsens as awkward and heavy as laden HGVs across rough terrain including wooded hills and swampy patches for, in the case of Stonehenge, over 200 miles (and a minimum of twenty for the 'local' stones near Marlborough) must surely have had some finished ideal to power it. Masons and navvies working on a medieval cathedral knew they would not live to see the final result, but they were being paid, had a job, were engaged in godly work, and had a concept (even if only on parchment) of what God's palace would look like. Sculptors of roof-bosses too high up to see with the naked eye lavished detail on them not just out of a craftsman's instinct and enjoyment but because the eye of God could see everywhere: it was a sensible decision arising out of their unquestioned belief in an after-life, in divine Judgement. The million man-hours estimated to have been consumed by the making of Silbury Hill would have needed more than a feeling that this sweaty toil was nourishing the soul, or the peculiar satisfaction that individuals get out of working as a crew (felt even in a time when individuality was a far weaker concept): if not some material reward, then a sense of edging towards some astonishing finality.

Nevertheless, to us it seems a touch lunatic. Take the dragging of the sarsens: even if this was done by their large, robust and shaggy cows (why not? – cattle are likely to have pulled ploughs and sledges), people must have died along the way, in the days before hard hats, harnesses and health and safety. *Stonehenge Decoded*, a recent National Geographic film documentary, reconstructs the epic journey, with handsome young men and women hauling the boulder on rolling logs and occasionally getting crushed, or attacked by enemy tribes. It is convincingly gruelling – and we're only talking about the shorter distance from the sarsen field of Fyfield Down, a trip still calculated to have taken many months. Each one an unrecorded odyssey with its own heroes and stories and villains. And all without a single mug of tea.

Lunacy is not just an action or a thought, it is an absence of the normal, of our own normality as well as theirs. Normality for us is, of course, entirely constructed from our own bias and prejudices. This very book risks normalising something extraordinary. As Julian Thomas, an archaeologist of a philosophical bent, states in *Understanding the Neolithic*: 'it is precisely through attempting to find out more about the past that we erode its unfamiliarity ... The difference of the past is inexhaustible.' Or, as a schoolfriend put it when I asked him for memories of Silbury Hill and the Mound: 'They were just there, and not objects of mystery or wonder ... Too much study, [and] they lose the matter-of-factness that for hundreds of years allowed them to just be.'

While I beg to differ on the mystery and wonder angle, I agree that the quality of being, its beautiful slow-rippling invisible waves, can be easily disturbed, easily crackled by our endless interference. The action of shifting those great stones only seems mad because we have lost the narrative, the context, the background matter-of-factness. There may even have been a real narrative behind it, a Homerian tale, in the sense of an old epic story involving heroes and gods. I hear drums and horns and chanting when I imagine each stone being levered up into place, slipping into its pit, hundreds hauling on the ropes: that, too, might have been part of the story. The god of stones holding the sarsen steady with one finger as he held the god of death at bay, the ashen terror flailing with all five fists in the great last battle.

Recently I returned to India after some fifty years: strong early memories of our life in Calcutta when I was a little boy were instantly recovered. My wife and I were lucky enough to attend a pre-Hindu Theyyam ritual near Kannur, on the Malabar coast. We arrived in a village by bone-shuddering auto-rickshaw at 3.30 a.m., then careered down a steep and winding track to the Hindu temple in front of which, in the sacred courtyard, a god was already dancing with a fiery torch. The Kolam had begun.

We were the only westerners, yet we were urged by the spectators to stand at the front – so close that when the frenzied attendants kicked the small red-hot heap of embers, it snowed around us. The men, dressed as gods in fantastic goggle-eyed masks and elaborate costumes, were in a trance state after weeks of fasting in isolation: this was a role they had inherited in a tradition that may originally date from Neolithic times, unique to the area around Kannur, and traditionally performed by the lower castes – an astonishing reversal of status in an unbending system.

They weren't playing the gods, of course, they were possessed by them, assuming their supernatural powers from the moment they looked into the mirror. Some dozen drums, cymbals and a plaintive horn kept up a ceaseless accompaniment, but what struck me was that the two gods merely bobbed and twirled gently in complex patterns, almost lumberingly: only humans jiggle about.

We moved after an hour or so to an adjoining, much larger area in which, to my astonishment, a simulacrum of Silbury Hill glowed: a huge mound of charcoal embers whose heat pulsed fiercely on our faces through the tropical night air. Onto this scorching tump, kept fired up by attendants with rakes, the two red-and-yellow gods were thrown repeatedly face forwards by means of flexible handles of cord, then abruptly tugged back until their voluminous skirts of coconut leaves had to be periodically doused by pails of water fetched from an oil drum next to us. Each shove onto the embers was accompanied by shouted chants from the attendants, raggedly pacing and dancing around the incandescent mound, but the spectators – hundreds of local devotees – watched in awed silence. The masked men looked like giant puppets when thrown and dragged off, but they were all too real.

When dawn came, I felt energised and extraordinarily positive.

Silbury as the simulacrum of a heap of glowing embers. Why not?

Later, I asked a man fishing for trout why the men did not get burnt during that particular Kolam. 'Because,' he said, as if it was obvious, 'they have the god inside them.'

Theyyam, with its fearful masks and danger and flickering light, is both an art form and a mystic rite. Each Kolam – there are hundreds – represents a different legend featuring gods and heroes: it is story-telling theatre, sacred ritual and fantastical dance combined. The one we attended, called 'Thee Chamundi', retells the story of Prahlada, the devout nephew of a demon king, cast into the fire by his uncle for worshipping Lord Vishnu, before the latter kills the demon. This is the kind of fleshed-out and verbal context that the prehistoric monuments have lost. We have only the debris of a vast imagination.

We have also lost the states of mind, induced or otherwise. We have lost the masks.

'A Mask is a device for driving the personality out of the body and allowing a spirit to take possession of it,' wrote Keith Johnstone in his remarkable book, *Impro: Improvisation and the Theatre*, which I devoured as a budding performer and recycled in my own teaching and still go back to regularly. I experienced something of this trance state when studying with the teacher and director John Wright, who was inspired by Johnstone to use half-masks made from life-size faces cut from glossy magazines and pasted onto card. The mask flows into your mind and your body and at first you are shorn of words, you struggle to speak, you become another. Later, at Desmond Jones's mime school, we learnt how to move like apes or early hominids (Jones had trained the actors in the Palaeolithic epic *Quest for Fire*, directed by Jean-Jacques Annaud), and I again fell into a trance state in which I was both inside and outside what one might call a body mask created purely by movement and posture. Meanwhile, with my theatre company, white face make-up let me look out at the world through a clown's eyes.

To comprehend the effort taken by those early builders, we need to remember how easily our bodies and minds can slip into other modes, parallel realities. Surmising from a desk in the twenty-first century can only take us so far. If those fantastic efforts have come down to us without the stories and myths and legends, without the vulnerable props made out of wood or vegetation, and above all without the everyday voices and remarks and jokes and mistakes, then our vision of them is even more distorted. These people must have felt powerful, clever – what we would now call cutting-edge – as they surveyed the progress of their great constructions. It would take a fierce twist of the imagination, however bleakly secular, to see these hard-labouring folk as desperate and credulous and sad, shoring up their sacred defences with an open-topped motte or a circular wall of giant boulders with hopeless gaps – slipping and floundering around uprooted rocks or up the sides of a mammoth mound when they should have been milking their animals or attending to hostile neighbours of flesh and blood.

Were the hauliers local clan members or drawn from the entire island? We come back to the depressing possibility that they were slaves. Did slaves not help to build the Pyramids at roughly the same time? Imagine the society that forced people to do such a thing, without any reward. Imagine the priestly terror, the whips, the cruelty of it all – if not perhaps as psychotically cruel as colonial slavery, with its Biblical justifications: Exodus declares that a man who beats his slave to death should not be punished if the victim survives 'for a day or two', and even Jesus seems to approve of severe thrashings. No wonder those who exercised their right arms on my own buttocks on several occasions over the years, for quite trivial faults, happened to be such devout believers. They weren't being hypocritical at all. If I couldn't sit down for the rest of the day, it was doing good to my soul.

Most gods, including the Christian god, have both angry and loving aspects, both destructive and protective. You are my chosen, if you don't annoy me. If you behave. Perhaps both were on display in the chalkland temples: the need to provide a sacred space to draw the gods or ancestors deeply into the communal space for their protective and nurturing powers, and the starker, nervously human need to appease. But what kind of supernatural entities could only be appeased by such superhuman effort – by tearing out great boulders that had stayed there in that spot for ever, left by the ice in one of the numerous periods of glaciation countless aeons before? Tearing them out with antler picks and ox shoulder blades and pure muscle and, perhaps towards the end, the helpful concept of leverage?

Was that how the Amesbury Archer, although doubtless somewhere high up in the prehistoric peerage, had his kneecap ripped off?

These days we lean towards the idea of a community effort, everyone in it together; voluntary work. And so it may have been: I say again, who could have coerced so many – or, at least in the case of Stonehenge, forced them to come

from so far? Or was it a mixture of the two? Do it or else –
and I don't even mean the kind of impaling that impressed
shirkers at Kandy. I mean the softly compulsory stuff like
having to go to school, or having to earn a living in front
of some mind-numbing factory belt, or having to mend that
washer on the tap. Not doing it may have made you an exile,
a pariah. Or, less heavily, doing it meant you brought honour
to your family, like fighting the Boche. The white feather of
refusal avoided. *England expects*…

Maybe each stone was mending a leak. A leak in the
universe. Stopping it up. Do it or else. Or else famine. Or else
the dead will rise all at once and wither us like grass, as the
priests predict. Look at the way the moon is racing so fast
above those clouds. Father saw the moon do that, once, and
the frost came for three weeks. Smell it on the wind. We need
to put that stone in. Or else.

They lived on the edge of terror, terror emanating from
both the ulterior woods and the god-streaked sky, from
both the other side of the hill and the lightless underworld.
Security was the name of the game. Endless systems-building.
Endless appeasing.

And in return: protection, nourishment.

Thirty years ago I'd have said: they lived on the edge of
extinction, a nuclear winter of the mind.

Each monolith a blank screen for our shadows.

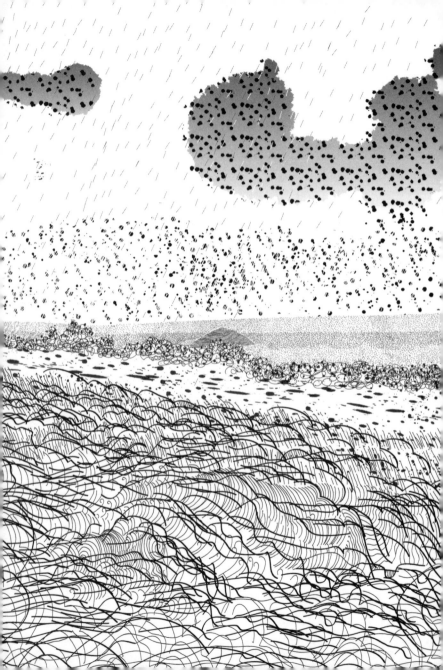

Seven

L ast year I was in the Avebury area for All Hallow's Eve, a time when the place gathers to its bosom a myriad of alternative believers: this is the big day for pagans, a day beginning at night. These are the first hours of winter by when, traditionally, all the harvest should have been gathered, firewood stacked, livestock brought in. This was the time when the gods approached Earth and the dead were almost touchable, returning home for one day in the year like prisoners on tight parole. Fires blazed out of the darkness in defiance of the coming tenebrous cold, beacons to the gods and spirits. Sacrifices were offered, human or animal.

Wiccans – as many modern-day pagans like to be known as – call it Samhain, acknowledging Halloween's Celtic roots and peeling it away as much as possible from Hallowmas, the three-day Christian observance when the faithful dead are remembered. This palimpsest of confused origins thickens the festival, itself overlaid in these post-rural times with commercial tat and currently geared largely towards children, for whom the chance to dress up as vampires or witches in fluro-green, or to go round menacingly to front doors for sweets, is irresistible.

I began the day at Silbury, of course.

It was very quiet, oddly, and the late October sky was milky and still, as if drawing its breath for winter. I walked from the little car park under the trees along the westerly track, struck for the first time by how beautiful the surrounds of Silbury are. I was looking past the hill, her outline hazed by the massed silvery-lilac panicles of false oat grass, towards Fyfield Down and Marlborough. There was an almost mystical sense of calm beatitude – meadows, low-lying fields, tufts of trees… perhaps, I thought, this is why this particular spot was first chosen as a sacred place – the centre of the centre.

Silbury, as ever, gathers the calm to herself, remaining completely obdurate in her indecipherability. This is the very reason I feel so intimate with her. She demands nothing. She is. What she gives is both entirely herself and entirely not herself, because we don't know what she is. So what we see in her is what we see in ourselves, only it's always a good vision because she absorbs what we are so entirely into her great grassy, uninterpretable and uninterpreting body. Wordless, she welcomes us in. As I walk to the end of the path, looking at her over the floodable field between, I feel better already. It has been a difficult year, and coming back to Silbury is always good therapy.

'In our department,' said a friend from Oxford recently, 'we have local historians and archaeologists who brood over Silbury.' I like the idea of experts brooding. There is something maternal in it. But perhaps Silbury broods, too.

Some fourteen years back, one calm morning soon after the deep hole was discovered in her top, I climbed her just as I did in the old days. The hole was surrounded by a wire fence and looked nasty, its sides rough as a tooth cavity, its width a good 7 feet, its depth even more. I thought of Hopkins again, and those painful lines from 'Binsey Poplars':

> Since country is so tender
> To touch, her being so slender,
> That, like this sleek and seeing ball
> But a prick will make no eye at all.

I looked out through the morning mist and felt maudlin, rather than energised. The sounds of the new century disturbed, sounded angry – a chainsaw, cars, a gunshot, the distant groan of a plane. The summit's hole seemed to suck my spirits down, fill me with darkness. It is harder than ever to achieve what Edward Thomas would find along lonely combes: 'pure earth and wind and sunlight – out of which beauty and joy arise, original and ancient, for ever young.'

A few steps away from the central dip and towards the north-east, near the edge, I suddenly felt dizzy, even migrainish, just as I had in the Hopi village decades before. I sensed, rather than thought, that this hill was, in some way, the surculose root-ball of the island's spiritual energies, propagating in a way we can no longer grasp or explain, sending out suckers of invisible information.

Then a beating sounded, approaching up the spiral path. I broke out in a sweat, my chest swirling with adrenalin.

Three, maybe four figures with feathered headdresses and face paint were hammering on drums a few yards off and a little down the slope, so that only their naked upper torsos were visible, slightly turned away and facing the view, as if playing to the massed, awestruck believers.

This episode lasted no more than fifteen or twenty seconds, while my head seemed to fizz as if full of sherbet, but it felt so like a time-slip that sometimes I think I may have had a glimpse of what happened up here: a crack opening, something granted, or perhaps the chasm joined.

It sounds coy, even cranky, but the above was precisely what happened.

I celebrated the moment by writing a somewhat caustic poem. I can still see them there, the glistening shoulders and the swaying feathers, half in and half out of my head.

Here again on All Hallow's Eve, I thought about that glimpse – an involuntary glimpse, perhaps, into my own mind. But it had made me feel stronger, safer, even chosen. Something special had been drawn out of me. Silbury, as cathedrals do, focusses the light like a prism, concentrates the imagination, draws down the supranatural spirit – God, or the gods – into the natural sphere of earth and stone where we can see it feelingly in its brilliant, refracted rays as something that exists.

This is real power. The Neolithic community would have felt similarly stronger and safer. By the time the hill was finished, it was visible from miles around. A great home for the spirit that would simultaneously have freaked out any competing neighbours.

That lot have the gods on direct call. They have the power. Look, see it beyond that brow? That white glimmer? Don't stare at it for too long, child. You'll attract attention. From the beyondsky, from the underrealm. We'll all go down. We'll all sicken and die.

How different is this reading from that of the Victorians and their Druidic imaginings, to whom great works of engineering were part of the thrust and seal of Empire? As Charles Knight put it in 1845:

> If it were a component part of the temple at Abury, [Silbury] is still to be regarded, even more than the gathering together of the stone circles and avenues of that temple, as the work of great masses of the people labouring for some elevating and heart-stirring purpose. Their worship might be blind, cruel, guided by crafty men who governed them by terror or by delusion. But these enduring monuments show the existence of some great and powerful impulses which led the people to achieve mighty things.

I want to put some distance between myself and this talk of manly, muscular, 'heart-stirring' purpose, but perhaps it's just as near the truth as any other interpretation. We need to remind ourselves again that the alluring smoothness of prehistory must have been as equally full of jagged megalomaniacs and suffering masses as the history we know about. The great mound of Alyattes in ancient Lydia, bigger than Silbury, was built for a man who, in life (according to Herodotus), would 'invade Milesian territory when the crops were ripe, marching in to the music of pipes, harps and… oboes', leaving the houses alone but destroying the trees and seizing the crops – and repeating this each year. His mound was funded by the people of Sardis.

The A4, the Bath Road, seems even more savage an intrusion, but I can deal with it: after all, I used it to get here, although for some reason I find the three-mile stretch between Marlborough and Silbury atavistically terrifying to drive – and I am not a nervous driver. Long after the road is gone, the tarmac puckered or torn or even absorbed entirely by the earth, the cars not even a distant memory of rusting hulks, Silbury will still be there. After all, a century after their manufacture, how many of those 15 million Model-T Fords remain?

I turn right towards Waden Hill, slipping along the hoof-churned path running alongside the Beckhampton stream that drains into the Kennet (*Cunnit* in ancient parlance) to the south. Keeping Silbury in view through the aspens and oaks that line the stream, I begin to climb Waden, now a protected slope of pasture.

As usual, Silbury grows in size, more dominant, more immense – but from whatever angle I look at her, she has a latent, brooding power. As I puff on up, she sinks beneath Waden's gradual crest, its wind-flattened tussocks combed dramatically towards me – although there is no wind: arriving from the other direction, her slow reappearance is always impressive, even disturbing. The buffeting growl of the A4 is hushed by distance: the view south to the horizon is magnificent.

The two bent hawthorn trees halfway down the hill on the northern slope, some 100 yards before you join Kennet Avenue's male-female stones at the bottom, are covered in offerings, including bright strips of cloth or ribbons tied in bows and wickerwork hearts fluttering and twirling in the breeze. This is not just because it is Samhain: despite the lurid polyester colours, I feel a pulse of gratitude. Cynics might say that modern paganism is a recent invention, a potpourri of elements drawn together and given a name less alarming than Witchcraft by a retired British civil servant, Gerald Gardner, in the 1950s. Yet paganism never disappeared, it was only suppressed, and sympathetic or homeopathic magic and animism are inevitably central to human consciousness in the context of a powerful and often bewildering nature; a nature we screen off through a distorting technology at the very time we are penetrating matter's innermost secrets, but which is in no way diminished in actual power.

My history teacher once explained that the Anglo-Saxons lived in a 'mythopoeic' world – that all natural phenomena were personified, that even a stone was 'Thou' rather than 'It'. Not the most focussed of students, I nevertheless woke up at this. I had no idea then that the term 'mythopoeic' was in itself recent, dreamed up by the philosophers Henri and Henrietta Frankfort in the 1940s to explain pre-modern thought. It's tough living in a world of abstract, impersonal laws; it's non-poetic, however amazing the stuff science tells us (more amazing than anything in myth, in fact, but that's not the point). The poetry of human existence has such deep roots that it must knock up against the white-coated laboratory view that has overlain it.

The garlanded trees turn my thoughts voluminously vatic, but bitten with an acid frustration. Our concrete, sensual perceptions have withered. The economic principles established by the purest creed of individualism have been nurtured by the greedy and the reckless – the 'cowboys', as my father would call that type – who are a handful compared to the numbers who will suffer (or are already suffering) from our tryst with the devil of profit, the most serious effect being human-induced climate change. The cowboys have stitched us up, bolted us into dependency, made us addicted to oil, gas, sugar, pharmaceuticals, what have you.

It is an extraordinary fact.

We need the gods back, we need to sacralise the planet – was it so naïve to personify nature, to fill it with spirit, if that taught us to honour her and even to fear her? Because she is fearful. She needs to be appeased – not with bloody sacrifices but with another kind of sacrifice: the killing of our blind arrogance. Then we can learn to love and adore her in all her majesty and intricacy.

But was it not a sort of human arrogance that built Avebury, Stonehenge, Silbury Hill? Those grand incursions on the trees, on the wilderness, on the sky? Each a god-like pact with the gods? A kind of mask-possession writ large: step into the circle, over the threshold, stand on the summit under the stars and bring the gods inside you?

I don't think it was the same species of arrogance, because there was also an implicit recognition of our essential smallness. I think it was an honouring, an acknowledgement of the greater powers of nature, of what we loosely call the cosmos. I haven't a shred of evidence either way, but these creations seem to occupy a quite different space from the industrial stripping of the planet's resources – still thought of in my childhood as heroic, but now as disastrous, unsustainable, to most sane human beings.

But somewhere deep down, perhaps there is a common root. One day maybe I'll wake up and see Silbury not as something beautiful and strange but as a demon lover, vexing my dreams of natural equilibrium, of walking the earth with a light tread.

Swollen and heavy, heaped out of the scoured ground by sheer human thew. Look at us. Look at what we can do. Forget your unchanging knapped flints, your hunter flickeriness. This is the age of copper. Of big herds. Of stuffed granaries, soon. This is permanence.

A child with its skull split. Two teenagers curled beside a stone.

In the wrong hands, nature fearful can become nature thirsty for blood.

I don't want to pursue this line of thought, yet I turn and retrace my steps up the slope a few feet to the point where her summit appears again out of the crest of Waden Hill. Just to check. She emerges like Venus from the waves. Utterly beautiful.

I come back down again, relieved.

These bent hawthorn trees draped with offerings make me think of a question my now-adult eldest son asked long ago: 'Where is God? Up in the sky, or in everything around us?' I said it was the latter, in my view. 'In every leaf?' 'Yes, definitely.' 'So if he's in every leaf, where does he actually stand?' 'Well he might actually be a lot of shes,' I murmured, unconvincingly. It certainly didn't convince Josh.

A lot of shes everywhere, in every leaf and blade of grass. But we still need special places where we can focus and intensify and channel.

I am walking towards one now, between a line of stones traced like an exaggerated birth canal. Almost certainly a processional route, the Kennet Avenue leads you towards Avebury's great mute circle through tussocky fields. I am almost alone. A dog runs in and out of the few stones left – male on one side, female on the other, or so we deduce from their respective pillar and diamond forms. There were hundreds making up the two Avebury avenues, but most have gone; smaller than the monoliths of the circle, the survivors are still impressive. Endless weeks of struggle were needed to drag them here and lever them upright.

There is perhaps a greater potency in this field-meandering avenue, despite the cars and lorries speeding down the parallel lane twenty yards away, than in the circle itself. It doesn't help the latter having a village in the middle, of course, with the A4361 cutting a zig-zag through and which is used by maniacs on some other time-level. Its beautifully tended hedgerow

visible in an 1890 photograph is now a barbed-wire fence. And Avebury, as part of the UNESCO World Heritage Site, receives around 350,000 visitors a year. It must have been a fraction of that in the early 1970s, but at least the dark days (in the 1980s) of a private medieval theme park with jousts and fluttering banners are long over.

English Heritage and the National Trust and even Wiltshire Council appear to be taking what the draft management plan calls 'a holistic and strategic approach' to the multiple pressures that this inconveniently sited temple faces, the most sensitive approach being to local farmers in a bid to shift from intensive arable to grassland. There is certainly improvement. Agribusiness no longer laps at these unprofitable sarsens, as it does at the Sutton Hoo mounds. The real problem lies in the millions of visitors to come.

The Avebury temple, with its great encircling bank and vast ditch, has a deep place in my heart: when I hardly knew my wife, back in 1982, I invited her to have a walk here, finishing with a pint in the Red Lion. We sat on the slope under the trees, looking down on the village from the northernmost point of the embankment, and she told me of her Polish-Jewish pedigree on the paternal side, that her brother was a Tibetan Buddhist... and other exotica as I studied the movement of her lips, love's weak-kneed underling.

Although a Londoner, she had known Marlborough from an early age (she was now twenty-one): her best friend, Sasha, was the granddaughter of the owner of the leather factory that I remembered very well – the stink of the hides at the back, the thrumming from the low building (it was soon to be knocked down for new housing.) Sasha's parents had a little brick-and-tile cottage in the grounds of her grandfather's house, the latter now sold off. Fresh from Cambridge, Jo was living in the cottage while she taught maths at the College for a term. I had returned to my old school for an undefined stretch – the pay and conditions were good, and I had been solicited at a moment when I was flat broke after several years with my itinerant downland theatre company. I felt a failure; the girl I had been pursuing for two years had definitively found someone else; and most traumatic of all, one of my closest friends from the College had just killed himself.

Avebury gave me Jo: this is why I find the idea of it as purely about death – about phantoms and the ancestors – difficult. When I was living in nearby Aldbourne on my own, touring the villages with puppets and mime, packing eggs to make ends meet, banging the proverbial medieval drum through festivals like the thankfully unelectrified Ecology Summer Gathering in Glastonbury, I wrote an interpretation of Avebury in a kind of evening trance – all but automatic writing, I suppose. The stone circle was conceived of as a prehistoric grinding-stone, examples of which I have stumbled on between the vines in drier Languedoc: a round quern-stone against which the handstone is turned, crushing the grain to flour. I wrote that you must walk round Avebury in a certain direction – anti-clockwise – and that this would grind out the husks within you, make you fruitful.

A year or so later, I walked round in this correct way with my future wife – widdershins, as it were. My insight into Avebury's function might have held more water had rotary querns come to the island with the late Neolithic, but they didn't: they arrived no earlier than 400 BC, replacing saddle querns that crush like a rolling pin or with a one-handed rocking motion. I didn't know that fact when I was dating, happily. And it did turn out to be fruitful, quite literally: two boys and a girl.

Equinox·
TRAVELLING· Theatre·

EQVINOX was shaped through windy
places·shadows and tall trees : with one ear
cocked on the village · equinox taps the
wisdom of children and foxes :

EQVINOX : a striving to revive the
rich life and rhythm of simple existence
before ga~ga machinery and media · in the
hope that pondering the innate of soil and
soul may bring a wide~eyed smile and
wondering :

EQVINOX : a banana fruit~cake
assembly team of loons and minstrels ·
all wrapped up in a hessian blanket :

EQVINOX travelling theatre ·
takes its medieval baggage of puppets
and madness through the remnants of the
countryside·playing anywhere inside or
out : True Thomas the Rhymer and
Starveling and sundry others act·dance·
sing·manipulate puppets and masks
and guitars and three~hole pipes and
tambours · and generally give all folk
a goodly time :

tel: hermitage (0635) 200792 ;

In other ways, too. Avebury acts as the portal to my several slim volumes of poetry.

The very first poem in my first collection, *Mornings in the Baltic*, relives a drama workshop for kids that we would now say was 'site-specific'. It was under the aegis of the Wiltshire Folk Life Society, run by a striking woman from the village with long silver hair, reminiscent of Joan Baez. Having seen one of our itinerant shows, she invited Equinox Travelling Theatre to perform in the Great Barn at Avebury, then housing a wonderful collection of old farming tools, and to follow it up with a week's workshop. I decided to use the stone circle as our Brookeian empty space, performing in what Stukeley called the 'Solar Temple', our locus the concrete marker that shows where the Obelisk once stood: this was a single thick stone felled in the Middle Ages and which Burl posits (from a burial found near it) was associated with the ancestors and death rather than fertility.

When the story ended the kids danced and laughed and it was one of the most satisfying moments of my life.

Drama Workshop, Avebury

After rehearsals in the village hall
the children took their cymbals, drums,
pipes and whistles, masks and costumes,

out into the centre of the ring
and began the performance: some the spirits
of the forest, some the destruction,

one who refused to be anything other
than his dog. Not much audience:
a gathering of helpers, a German couple

who wondered if it was traditional,
the local custom. No, I said.
There was a light drizzle, and the sheep

ignored us. The few upright stones
leaned like those old, kindly men
in parks, always vaguely interested

in what is going on. The ridge
swept round enormous behind the houses.
Drums and cymbals and humming and cries

and one eight-year-old running
to the ridged horizon, instead
of turning for the happy finale.

She explained afterwards, dazed and panting –
'There's too much space,' sweeping her hand;
and returned to orange in plastic cups.

I'm glad this poem begins my published cursus; it somehow contains everything I've been trying to do since. What the child said still strikes me as profound: the stone circle creates its own space, a space that has nothing to do with normal space. The circle of infinity concentrates our attention on above and below, like a tube, a microscope or a telescope. Above, it really is more or less infinite. And below?

My good friend Peter, who played God in a shabby eighteenth-century coat in Equinox's performance of the medieval mystery cycle, worked with a group of young people with severe learning disabilities. One hot moonlit summer's night he took them to Avebury. Impish, autistic Sean danced around the stones giggling and laughing. In the car going back, Carl, who was autistic and echolalic – meaning that he only repeated what you said to him, or stock phrases he had learnt over the years – suddenly leaned towards Peter and whispered, 'Rabbits of moon lake'. This was not a stock phrase, nor had anyone ever said it to him. I remember Carl would sit and laugh to himself, moving his head as if someone was stroking it. And then he would spring up and go into one of his routines and occasionally whisper *rabbits of moon lake* again to himself. 'The guys who were on the autistic spectrum were always at their most expressive when the moon was high,' Peter recalls over thirty years later. 'Strange place, Avebury.'

Rabbits of moon lake.

As a teenager some years before, I came here on a warm June evening for our art teacher's leaving party, and the stars blazed towards the end of what was a Watteau-like *fête galante*. The ditches were perfect for roly-polies down their slopes – we were still young enough to be child-like but in a knowing, ironic way. What I most remember was the way the huge sweeping banks dwarfed us, making us seem sparsely scattered as we partied into the gloam.

When the circle was intact, it must have captured the stars, a focus for their power. Neolithic people had no conception of what the sparkles in the night sky actually were, of course, and their interpretations – holes in a black lid, divine eyes, gods' camp fires, whatever – remain lost to us. But the constellations' enthralling mystery may have been shifted by the circle of stones into something more personal and intimate: to step over the threshold of ordinary space into the temple's space is to transform both yourself and your relationship with the physical world. Looking at the stars from within Avebury's stones perhaps was, in some way, an act of poiesis – a making of something new and transcendent but without leaving the body or the earth.

A poem-making out of matter and time and your own flesh and spirit... only possible because of the lens, the concentration of the lens, that is the Avebury eye – or rather (from a high-up hawk's point of view, with the henge's two inner circles still intact), a pair of eyes complete with irises in a moon face, reminiscent of the mouthless Neolithic statuary found in our area of France. Up she once stared, goggle-eyed, at the twinkling gods. A huge mask, like the Dorset Ooser's we would prance behind in our shows.

The genius of the buried stones is that they go down as well as up: digging out the shaft, the socket, into which the haft was lowered must have made this very clear. As a number of scholars have suggested, it is a reconciliation – of the underworld and the overworld, of earth and sky. Amidst the minimal technology of the times (however skilled their nimble fingers), it must have been striking how a tall post, a great unwieldy stone, could be held firm by depth, by the soil's grip. Physical laws were not understood conceptually, but read as mimetic acts, one by one, unique to themselves. The stone or the post was being rooted, like a tree. And the stones' roots held firm for 4,000 years, until deracinated by greed and fanaticism.

Gap-toothed Avebury, like a god or goddess punched in the mouth, is a metaphor for our own rootless – toothless – times, where the immense poietic power of circles has been appropriated by management consultants and marketing teams: orange in plastic cups. As with everything from Shakespeare to Anfield, we now have 'the Avebury Experience' – the capitalisation by some PR agency of what is a personal encounter (banal, intense, whatever) feels like the ultimate junk call on meaningfulness, perhaps on life itself.

I don't quite remember the farm as dung-strewn and tractor-clattering, but now, as the HQ of the Experience, it is busy in another way. Especially today: a tent is offering make-up sessions, and gaggles of black-lipped children in cloaks and broad-brimmed hats, some entirely hidden behind furry werewolf heads or plastic skull masks, are being herded along by parents. The ancient festival of Halloween is now Gothic fun, and a worldwide money-spinner.

The great old threshing barn has not been the Wiltshire Folk Life museum and study centre for a long time. The present National Trust museum is geared to a younger audience: its displays and screens ('Being Neolithic' and so on) are child-friendly, if occasionally stating the painfully obvious: '*The day and night sky, and the world under their feet seem to have been important to Neolithic people.*' Maybe we do need to be told this, saturated by the virtual as we are. Gallant efforts are made to bridge the gap between knowing something and actually grasping it: '*Picture your own ancestors living in Avebury when the stone circles were built. These distant relatives would have been your great, great, great, great…*' – I count 200 of them, which seems a little pat, but it is striking how that verbal chain evokes a link with people impossibly distant just at the same time as it renders it meaningless.

This teacherly high jinks does, however, distract from the superb interior – all tie beam trusses, haunched posts, raked struts, purlins, windbraces and cruck blades.

I find to my surprise that Avebury Manor, previously inaccessible, has been entirely done over by the BBC and the National Trust for a programme called *The Manor Reborn*, in which the place was refurbished to reflect its 500-year history. Although the grey-haired guides are heavily into visitor participation, and the kitchens are full of eager children stirring authentic copper bowls and crushing peppercorns with period pestles, the place resembles a series of studio sets, with big cut-out black cats and spiders marring the lovely gardens outside. I seek refuge in the near-empty Alexander Keiller Museum in the old stables.

There is always something reliable about bones and pottery and flint tools, as long as they are the real thing: here is the oldest pottery found in Britain – a cooking pot, 6,000 years old, that the marmalade millionaire dug out of one of Windmill Hill's huge grassed ripples. He also found the skeleton of a three-year-old child, henceforth nicknamed Charlie: recently the Council of British Druids wished him (or her) to be reburied, but were politely rebuffed. The skull's slipped jaw gives it an agonised expression.

As usual, the huddled old grey church gives me the impression of holding out inside the enemy camp. We performed one of our shows – the Norse myth of Balder – in its lovely Saxon nave; I had a raging temperature, head buzzing from 'flu. The tub font has a locally cut twelfth-century carving of Christ trampling on two dragons – evil and sin – yet our show starred the old pagan gods, including that cunning trickster Loki: furthermore, it went well.

The door creaks wide. None of the heat of that evening remains. A well-behaved smell of beeswaxed oak and cool plaster.

My subsistence strategy consists of soup, banana cake and tea in the NT café. I watch a pair of thatchers toiling cheerily on the barn roof and then, buffeted by too much Halloween mirth, head back by the north circle.

The present is too much with me, but on the other hand

the present is usually OK, ordinary in a friendly way – at least in the depths of the English countryside. The undulating ditch on the north-east quadrant seems even broader and deeper than on my last visit some months before: a gentle combe that is a time-grassed, more comforting version of the original. The sides would have been sheer-sliced white when new, and the albuminous outer bank of chalk rubble was so high it would have hidden the horizon – imprisoning, concealing, with only a walkway of green turf at the wall's base before the neck-breaking plunge into the ditch. The earthwork alone took so long – many decades, probably – that grass had started to felt the first stages before the rest was being finished at the far arc of the circumference.

On completion, at any rate, the central plateau would have been protected from the malefice of the ordinary world when it came to erect the outer circle of stones. Not just the bad, but the mundane: judging from the absence of gnawed bones in the debris of the great feasts (deliberately left, it seems), no dogs were allowed in the sacred spaces.

The ditch was achieved with antler picks, ox shoulder-blades and tough rope-hauled wickerwork baskets. My mother was carrying one of those – solid, square – when a car rammed into her on Chesham High Street's zebra crossing in 1966: the basket was crushed to a few inches, absorbing most of the impact so that all she had was a livid bruise on her thigh. 'The basket saved your leg, if not your life,' said the doctor. Her failing eyesight was not to blame, this time.

A well-known photograph in the museum shows Harold St George Gray's excavation in 1922 – a photograph which inspired a chapter in *Ulverton*. Labourers with rolled-up sleeves and dark waistcoats stand with their spades and

AVEBURY.
FOSSE. CUTTING IX, 1922.
(THE DEEPEST PART).

picks on four levels down to the ditch bottom, where a tall ladder is defeated by the depth of nine metres. It is nothing more than a giant trench, of course – the muddy mess on the surface recalling the Western Front for many of these men. Everything about the photograph speaks of another age, from the antique wheelbarrows to the men's caps and hats, yet it is a grass-blade's thickness away from us compared to the Neolithic. My grandmother was already a working woman in 1922.

Avebury's earthworks make an irregular circle, in fact, as if drawn freehand by a child: Burl considers the area they enclosed as not necessarily empty of barns, cattle enclosures or even houses, which would have made cord-measurement hard. I have long considered how one of the tiring factors of modern life is the perfection of its lines and the absolute regularity of its forms. Yet the small Roman temple in my home city of Nîmes – the best-preserved anywhere, erected by Augustus in memory of his two late nephews – is breathtakingly beautiful and completely regular and classical. We sense it was made by hand, built not in shuttered concrete or industrial brick but in blocks of local stone.

Industrialism involved a dehumanisation, of course: that was part of its point. Avebury and Silbury are both very human and completely other: this makes them moving. This makes them match the mystery of our brief bird-lives, appearing from one dark otherness and vanishing into another after a single flash of warmth and light.

The clear afternoon shows Silbury's distant summit reassuringly level with the horizon, small as a dark mouse between the tree-tops. I walk slowly past the vast flat flank of the 'female' Diamond Stone by the northern entrance, summoning up courage to cross the waspish little road by the stile further south. A teacher is lecturing a handful of sixth-formers. It is all about size and weight: at 65 tons, the stone is Avebury's heaviest, but perched on one of its angles like an ogress determined to practise ballet. It pierced half a metre deeper than its intended shaft, and has stayed put since, without an inch of a lean to it. The leather straps presumably keeping it steady as it was finally slipped in must have made a cobweb with a lot of struggling and straining flies, unless these people really did call on some lost telekinetic powers. A friend single-handedly fitting a massive stone sill for his fireplace used the gradual stepping-up method, inching the beast up with inserted planks resting on a scaffold. 'You can lift anything that way,' he said. 'You just need time and patience.'

There were no time-and-motion constraints in the Neolithic: you poured time into this bottomless bowl of work, that was half the point. It's the equation familiar to obsessive craftspeople, to certain artists, to painters of model figurines. It is Millais painting *Ophelia*, six long days a week on a chilly riverbank for five months.

Charles II visited Avebury in 1663, in the company of John Aubrey – a Wiltshireman to whose curiosity we owe not only *Brief Lives*, the famous set of gossipy biographical sketches, but also the first plans and descriptions of the monument before the stone-smashers had made too many inroads. His Highness was impressed by the bulk of the two right-angled Cove stones in the north-east sector, as he was by the minuscule size of the snails he noticed when climbing Silbury on the same day in 1663, having 'cast his eie' on her as she lay 'about a mile off'.

Aubrey provides us with the first little sketch of Silbury: looking like an upturned flowerpot in a neat circular bed, the

drawing shows the Bath Road and the *Fluvius Kynet* below *Selbury* or *Silsbury hill*. For all its dashed-off feeling, it does show the same path that was used until recently, ascending on the southern flank. Aubrey scribbled in his notebook, 'The country folk do call it Zelbury Hill and tell a story that it was raised over King Zel's grave.' I love the oral survival of the Wiltshire burr in that spelling: you can smell the wool, feel the rough hands, see the browned, cracked faces and the mouths opening to missing teeth. All those stories, all that knowledge evaporated for good. Language you could chew on. Language with the wind and rain blowing through.

I cross into Avebury's north-east sector – the most mutilated of all, with less than ten stones surviving, three of them fallen – wondering why Charles or any subsequent monarch didn't simply ban the destruction of, in Aubrey's words, 'these mighty stones (as hard as marble)' and 'so rude that they seem rather natural than artificial'. Although asked by His Majesty to dig at their base for human bones, he 'did not do it'.

I then spot something odd happening in the expanse of

bare grass beyond the Cove. Three men – one adult and two teenagers, really – are marking out a circular labyrinth with salt. I ask them what is going on. 'It's for tonight's ceremony,' says the older man, well-fleshed and with a Manchester accent. 'We're getting in touch with the dead. The veil between the life world and the death world is pretty thin, anyway, but tonight it gets so thin that the dead can pass through it and walk among us. That's what it's all about. The dead coming home.' I nod, looking appreciative. 'It's not scary,' he goes on, 'it's just how it is, it's natural. Then we're doing a procession down the Avenue and past Silbury to Swallowhead Spring, with our apples, and we're going to cast them into the river. It's all very friendly. There'll be fire,' he adds, indicating the two lads, who grin enthusiastically. 'There'll be a load of fire and drums and so forth.'

'What time does it start?'

'Oh, after the sun's gone down,' he says vaguely. 'It has to be dark, you see.'

This cheers me: it seems as genuine an article as you can get. Wiccan or whatever, I haven't asked. The living and the dead do seem to be separated only by the thinnest of veils, but what a veil, what a thinness, a kind of impenetrable millimetric cling-film membrane against which the dead faces press themselves and never make it through, however deeply you're grieving. There are many, many more dead than living – or there should be, given the millions of years that humans of one sort or another have been perishing, but maybe statistically this is no longer true. The world's population is now seven billion breathing souls, and rising by over two per second.

By the time I make my way round to the gigantic pair of

sarsens guarding the southern entrance, I feel overwhelmed by what I know, what we all know. Seven billion people, and nearly nine billion Earth-type planets in our galaxy alone, one for each person with room to spare. And there are billions of galaxies in the known universe. Maybe, in the days when I thought I was in contact with aliens, I wasn't being so crazy after all. Except that the closest Earth-like planet is probably around 70 trillion miles away.

All manner of numbers, and no sense.

A young couple are facing each other in front of the right-hand stone of the pair. The man has Ötzi's fur cap, his pigtail offsetting a blue cagoule; he rests his right hand on the woman's arm and the other on the small of her back, talking earnestly. Then he closes his eyes and she stands facing the stone, straight and concentrated, no doubt drawing on its energy field, tuning in to its resonance frequencies, whatever. It's a very private ritual. Her long chestnut-blonde hair tumbles over a hooded blanket-cape. That they aren't in white Druidic robes with silver hair or in black robes with dyed-black hair makes it more poignant, somehow.

They are ordinary, just as the Neolithic believers were ordinary once. Our world isn't ordinary, it's been made very strange. To combat this strangeness, we go back to the common sense of stone: to the rough surface of that sarsen, warmed by the sun or cooled by rain, deep-pocked by palm-roots millions of years ago, its extraordinary nuances of green and blue and cream, the odd splotch and dribble of black like a gutter-stain that, close up, turn into the Celtic knots and whorls of rare lichens, with the suggestion of a fossil towards the top, the monolithic facelessness broken only by a sudden brow ridge without an eye. The subtlety of unevenness!

I wish good luck to them under my breath and head back down the Avenue, keen to reach Swallowhead Spring while it is still light, going the way perhaps the ancestors did, from stone temple to earthen belly: rebirth, the spectacular rise of the belly as Waden's crest was crossed. Or perhaps not. Perhaps none of this. Perhaps just the gurgle of a child's throat as the copper knife crossed it. A dog scampers about between the stones, oblivious in the freedom of the field. The tracksuited owner barks at it to return.

Skirting Silbury by the east side, I hurry over the A4's self-important tarmac and onto the track that leads you up to the ridge and to West Kennet Long Barrow. After a few yards of this rutted, munching way, I veer off across an 'open access' field, once a managed water meadow and, hidden at an even deeper depth of time, the teeming Roman settlement conjured by a recent geophysical survey which showed, like an X-ray, a web of streets, alleys and house plots with hypocaust heating systems. This is unlikely ever to be fully excavated: the relevant authorities reckon that it would turn the area into an even hotter spot for tourists, necessitating a new infrastructure and destroying what calm still remains around the Neolithic sites. Presumably that's what it was in the first place: noisy, a busy staging post on the way between the sacred waters of Aquae Sulis and Londinium. Meet the gods, have a massage, drink from the ritual wells, buy some knick-knacks. The whinnying of horses, the murmurings of whatever solemn masses were performed to the gods before the hill's votive temples, stuck into the great, ancient flanks like tiny coins or nestling around its southern base, in view of where I am now.

The spring, part-source of the River Kennet, lies beyond the corner of the field and over some large sarsen stepping stones and a little wooden footbridge. The immediate area is a beautiful haven of slender reeds and old leaning willows with

a Rackham-like suggestiveness of unearthly creatures. The usual pagan offerings – ribbons and wickerwork pentangles – dangle between the leaves. Almost 300 years ago, Stukeley claimed the locals 'make merry with cakes, figs, sugar and water fetch'd from the *Swallow-head*… This spring was much more remarkable than at present, gushing out of the earth, in a continued stream. They say it was spoil'd by digging for a fox who earth'd above…' There is certainly no sign of water today, only a scoured serpent of gravel and sand between tussocks and the green-silvery reeds.

The upper Kennet rises seasonally from its source, its two springs dry until early spring. A lot of visitors must be disappointed, especially as the dry season has extended dramatically in recent years. Swindon absorbs 85 per cent of the upper Kennet's water, pumped up through bore-holes and supplying around 40,000 households – and not a drop comes back. Plans to reduce what is called 'over-abstraction' (Thames Water's licence allows for 45 per cent more) have met a funding wall. According to a report by the World Wildlife Fund, it is reckoned that the 'perennial head of the Kennet has moved about five miles downstream... to Marlborough.'

It is also reckoned that, in Neolithic times, ground water was some 16 feet higher, and an unmanaged Kennet meandered slowly over ground full of seeping springs, its source not at Swallowhead but – wait for it – in the middle of Avebury. The brooks we see now around Silbury are canalised, artificial. And this is all according to expert hydrologists, not New Age mystics: Silbury would have been in her watery element. Protected, and protecting.

Why otherwise build her in a low-lying, spongy valley?

Every few years, it still rains enough in the winter to fill her surrounding ditch: the archaeologist Mike Pitts took photos after a very wet 2012, showing Silbury astride her own

perfect mirror-shape, suggesting great depth in a marshy shallowness. The traces of two bridges on the south side of the ditch suggest such flooding was once a semi-permanent phenomenon. Given the imminence of undue climate change, it may become so again: the effect has been repeated in 2014.

Swallowhead is, at any rate, a withered relic. 'The nymphs are departed', as Eliot put it in *The Waste Land*, musing on the Thames. No nymphs here either… unless the two middle-aged women in jeans and blue cagoules, pink-dominated wellies and generous beaded shawls are a canny update. They are talking excitedly by the largest sallow whose low, thick branch necessitates a propitiatory dip of the head. The spring has been a popular pilgrimage site for years, particularly since Michael Dames's book proposed Silbury as the 'pregnant' Earth Mother and Swallowhead 'as Cunt' (not surprising, given the local name for the Kennet – 'Cunnit'). Springs were precious things in the days before piped water, of course, and accrete holiness or sacredness like moss, but cave-springs in particular are, in Dames's words, a 'sexual… symbolic amalgam'.

With Silbury's flooded ditch, we probably have an amalgam of the aesthetic and the metaphysical. The sheer power of the vision (a doubled hill, the dart of sunlight on water or rippling over the chalk-white flanks, the eerie shimmer of the moon) would keep evil spirits out, not on the assumption that evil can't swim but that water is in itself holy because life-giving and baptismally renewing and, perhaps, simply because of what Turner loved it for: its liquidity of light.

Dames notes that the ditch stretches or widens out of the circle on the west side like the head of a Palaeolithic 'Venus' figurine, but according to David Field, a more cautious archaeologist, this 'extension…, if water-filled, would have served as a cistern or reservoir. Elsewhere in the world, cisterns have often been the focus of ritual and ceremony. The mirror-like quality of standing water may have had symbolic implications too.' Water is a community's most precious commodity: the physical and the sacral were in unison here, mutually dependent. Some years ago I climbed Silbury when the westerly meadows below were sheened in places with water, reflecting a perfectly blue morning sky rinsed by storm. It seemed quite obvious that the Hill was, in some ways, a holy island.

So I have no problems with this aquatic theory, although it makes one marvel yet more at the Neolithic ability to sculpt the landscape (with the simplest of tools) in a way that makes modern Land Art look puny. Glastonbury Tor, a natural conical mound that once rose out of the naturally flooded Somerset flats (drained in the fourth century), might have served as a prototype – especially given its ancient importance as a sacred site, continued in the legend of the holy spring that burst forth from the spot where Joseph of Arimathea buried the Holy Grail… at the cave-like entrance to the Underworld, tellingly.

Although the Kennet is no Ganges, the Thames may well have been. And the Kennet is a tributary of the Thames – one of over thirty. Jim Leary and others posit that Silbury might therefore mark the southernmost source of the great sacred river, the watery fount of creation to the clans round about, although whether they ever travelled the waters to their swirling conjunction with the North Sea at London Stone is unknown. We don't even know for sure that the great brown artery was, in fact, ever regarded as holy. It has been a poetic metaphor or symbol for many things: renewal, eternity, time, redemption, greed, morality, death, even sin and corruption – with all of these swirling together in Dickens's *Our Mutual Friend* – but evidence of ritual practice on its banks is more elusive. The Thames has accreted such a depth of historical silt that, to our eyes, it has a kind of sacredness anyway.

Chalk streams are transparent – 'gin clear' as fly fishermen say – and the Kennet is no exception. An elderly friend, a Hebridean called Mary, who spun and dyed her own wool and lived hand-to-mouth in a tiny converted chapel, showed me, back in my puppetry days, how to pick meadowsweet for yellow dye: the bankside clusters along the Kennet, flowing clear and smooth past the chapel, were so fragrant I felt drugged on sweetness.

Now its health is severely challenged by the malignities of firms like Bayer and Sygenta, manufacturers of neonicotinoids and other insecticides as ugly as their unpronounceable names. They leach into streams and rivers and, even at EU-permitted levels, 'wipe out half the invertebrate species you would expect to find in the water', as George Monbiot stated in a recent piece in *The Guardian* that specifically used the Kennet as example. This is simple chemistry: perhaps only science can save us from its own undrinkability, but will anyone listen? Most of us are scientifically illiterate. We need something more. Colin Tudge, in his magisterial book *Trees*, suggests reverence. 'Science in the service of appreciation, and appreciation in the service of reverence.'

And action, perhaps. *Media vuelta.*

The two women are holding large, flat drums. Goatskin, they tell me: one drum's tautness is painted with four trees depicting the different seasons, their roots meeting to make a circle in the middle. Robin and Kim, who are about my vintage, are excited because, when taking a photograph of the spring a few moments before, the digital screen had been obscured by a deep-blue ectoplasmic presence that wobbled about for a bit and then floated off. They both saw it, although I'm not sure if it was also visible off-screen. Being a Buddhist in the pre-Tibetan Bon tradition, with its roots in indigenous animism and sympathetic magic, Robin is certain that it was Menlha, the Bon medicine deity.

I step towards the spring with warnings to be careful. I like my new friends, they are friendly and enthusiastic and they welcomed me when they might have resented a male presence. The welcome intensified when I told them that I had known the area from boyhood, and had a thing about Silbury: I was recognised as one of their own. I have always been susceptible to the tofu-knitting, yoghurt-weaving world. There are degrees of flakiness, of course, defined by the usual criteria which might apply to anything from railway modelling to fundamentalist Islam: taking it too seriously, going on about it, being blind to any other mode of belief. Hitler and Himmler, remember, were worryingly flaky, keen on stone circles, vegetarianism, Arthurian legends, dark forests and fire ceremonies. That should keep us all on our toes when we wish the world back to a New Age version of the Neolithic – as I often do in the middle of the night, weary and even frightened of the hard-edged, cynical, reckless, profiteering, unequal, unbalanced, greedy-lying-bastards etcetera etcetera universe we have trapped ourselves in (or been trapped in by others), bereft of poetry and wisdom. Carl Jung, another of my early heroes, put it succinctly: 'The real natural man is just in open rebellion against the utterly inhuman side of life.'

The great question is whether the 'real natural man' is the bully with the metal-studded boots or whether our inner needles quiver towards the magnetic north of compassion and love. It depends on what the conditions are, and on what influences come to bear, and on what is trickling down from the top: money or ideological lunacy seem to be the present alternatives (perhaps they are two aspects of the same thing).

There is also blind stupidity. At least since the 1970s, we've verified that pumping carbon dioxide into the atmosphere is a crazed chemical experiment with inevitable, catastrophic consequences. Orwell, in his great wartime essay on socialism, *The Lion and the Unicorn*, berated the way the 'old and silly' in authority ignored the clear danger of Hitler throughout the 1930s, and had a term for those of his countrymen who admired Hitler and denied his evil intentions: 'obscure lunatics'. What better term for the climate-change denialists and those organs of the media that concur, even when not funded by Exxon and numerous other vested interests? What better term for those who see only benefit – a boost in Arctic tourism, new access to fossil fuels…

Kim and Robin, while enthusiastic, have kept their sense of humour and, though the conversation has strayed to the above as a corollary to the parched spring, we can crack a joke or two. I feel in good company. I feel at home. This is helped by the fact that, as I advance towards the cave-spring, they 'drum' me on, quietly and steadily, 'to protect and guard me'.

Apart from the lack of water, readers of Michael Dames's book must continue to be as confused as I was on my first visit to the spring, many years ago: his 1970s photograph shows a clear 'horseshoe shape... defined by the natural chalk wall,' in which the seeping, vulva-like tunnel outflow is clear of growth. Now the chalk is covered in thick grass and sedge, with a flat stone half-concealing the hole – a mantelpiece for votive knick-knacks. I lift my tiny digital camera and notice on its screen a tussock with a blue tint to the left of the hole.

I tell the women on my return, showing the result. The shade of blue has faded to the mere suggestion of a nuance, and Robin scoffs in her New Zealander's lilt. 'Ours was really, really blue, and took up almost the whole screen, *hovering*.'

Kim is a local and tells me the story that her father would tell her when she was small. A cobbler sits on a huge heap of shoes he's busy mending when the dragon arrives (it usually features the Devil, but this was a kid's version). The latter asks how far it is to Marlborough, which he wishes to incinerate. 'It's so far,' the cobbler replies niftily, 'that coming back I've already worn out all these shoes.' The dragon turns round and is never seen again. The pile of shoes turns into Silbury Hill.

This is, in fact, a delightfully garbled version of the traditional folk tale told about Silbury: the Devil was carrying a huge spadeful of earth that he wished to dump on Marlborough, and threw it aside when hearing the cobbler's cunning reply. It was the spadeful of earth that became Silbury. But I think Kim's dad's version is more evocative: Silbury blurring into the battered traces of a long journey. Worn-out soles, as it were.

This leads us into a discussion about the 'Bosnian pyramids' and the claim by one Semir Osmanagic, a Houston metalworking executive, that these natural hills – very much the same shape as Silbury – were constructed by the Illyrians around 12,000 BC as regulators of cosmic energy, bringing (I have since looked him up on the Web) 'the Earthly frequency... into accordance with the vibrations of our Sun.' He also believes that Hitler and his cronies escaped to an underground base in Antarctica. Osmanagic is quite clearly loopy, but Kim and Robin attended a lecture by him and were seduced.

One of the drawbacks of the alternative belief scene – as true back in the rune-loving 1920s as now – is that the sky's the limit: you can float off anywhere and lose any grip on what is called 'reality'. Flying above the clouds, you can believe the clouds are a solid, sparkling snowscape. Given 'reality' is itself relative and made up of a complex dance between the subjective and the objective worlds, now complicated by a plethora of virtual realities (the mimetic quality of video games, for example, is remarkable), we can't really talk about a single reality anyway. As Jung also maintained: 'Fantasy has a proper reality ... It is of course not a tangible object, but it is a fact nevertheless. It is a form of energy that becomes measured ... Psychic events are facts, are realities. When you observe the stream of images within, you observe an aspect of the world.'

Offering-trees, painted drums, healing megaliths, water guardians and earth energies proffer a much more enticing land of hidden powers and potentials as well as protection – a poiesis only you and a choice circle are privy to. I have already alluded to the period in my life when this sort of thing took over completely and I went narcissistic and paranoid, prelude to a breakdown: I am still uncertain whether being exposed to certain currents of fey thought lured me in too deep or whether other factors were chiefly responsible – the dicey transitional phase between childhood and adulthood, Oxbridge academicism and competitiveness, my mother going blind (the effects of a Japanese drug for dysentery that was being tested in India), a dose of opium-laced hash... But it was touch and go. It is so easy to believe you have been chosen, whether by God or extraterrestrials.

On the other hand, creative freedom plays necessarily close to the tumbled fence of lunacy. Great poetry of whatever style and content imbibes of the unconscious, the shaman's trance voyage, the cauldron of Ceridwen's intoxicating potion, Awen – three drops of which grant poetic inspiration, the fourth death by poisoning. W.B. Yeats's poetry would not have been the same without Mrs Yeats's (fraudulent) automatic writing, providing him with a coherent, if completely erroneous, symbology... but it could have been fatal to his talent.

The problem remains that those with a clear personality disorder find a kind of siphonable justification in this world, a kind of mirror-reflection of their own baleful visage, and tend to fool others with a vision whose cosmic breadth is usually in inverse proportion to its propagator's personal egotism. Gurus abound, as they always have done, vatic or vacant or both.

As I leave Swallowhead, Kim and Robin 'drum me out'. Wicca drumming tends to be a slow, rhythmic thudding like a magnified heartbeat, collectively enthralling and an expression of togetherness as well as of more cosmic matters: as I walk across what was once, if briefly, a Technicolor Roman town and is now nothing but tussocks, the fading beat rising from the trees behind seems to push me gently forward, cradling me, giving me a subtle strength. I am touched by the way it continues, almost inaudible, until my speck of a figure reaches the track on the far side.

This, I think, is genuine caring.

The deracinated Sanctuary looks slightly better in twilight.

Its traces lie on the spur of Overton Hill, a mile or so to the east of Silbury, just off the Bath Road and the Ridgeway. The concrete markers grow hazed and glimmering, like floating coffins, the knee-high post in the middle bearing a rosy apple, a wreath of sycamore leaves and some Golden Delicious settled around it (an alternative name for Samhain is Feast of Apples, and I remember fruitlessly bobbing for apples during childhood Halloweens).

Waden Hill's great belly dominates the view to the west, the red and white lights of cars threading beneath. A few yards off, an impressive group of bell and bowl barrows cluster, traversed both by the A4 and the far more ancient Ridgeway; three of the barrows are Romano-British, as if the sacred vibes were considered as operational into historical times. As from so many places on the Ridgeway, which rises due north from here before curving gently east on the crest of Hackpen Hill and up past Barbury Castle, Silbury's summit is visible, still as odd as ever: she is the head to Waden's torso, brow touching the skyline.

Trying not to curse the Farmer Greens of this world yet again, trying to think positive, I watch the sun setting beyond Waden and the darkness thicken towards All Hallows: what if, as that sentence mimics, time and place are not divided in our minds? What if that lumpen head out there contains all the time it took to build it, not in abstract terms but in the actual matter of clay and flint and turf and silt and chalk and sarsen? Don't we say, even now, 'I put a lot of hours into that'? There was no piece-work or hourly rate in the late Neolithic: there was no money. So time was not bound up with monetary value, nor was it measured precisely. The closest I come to this myself is when writing poetry, which in the case of certain individual poems has taken decades, on and off. So how did Neolithic folk view time? Maybe, in one sense, they never viewed it at all, not as something abstract or separate. Time was merely effect: a fading flower, the sun touching the hill, a distant memory. An accumulation of chalk. Maybe time didn't bother them, as such.

The building went on for decades, perhaps a century or more: Mike Parker Pearson reckons it would take a thousand people working full-time for two years to build a modern version. But this calculation is itself modern: as Jim Leary pointed out, those who started the whole thing with a heap of gravel on the ground surface could not 'possibly have known what the final manifestation of the monument would appear like or the phases that it would go through or that it would take several generations to complete'. They might, however, have guessed what they would be seeing from the summit if they kept it going long enough: by standing on Waden Hill. The future not as time but as view, or as a self-propelled ascent towards the gods.

The chalk-white dome resting in its flooded ditch, its own moat or perpendicular lake, perfectly reflected on a still, clear day, would have seemed to have been descending as well as ascending: remember the vertiginous magic of staring into a large puddle and seeing the sky, the deep-down tree-tops, the swimming birds? A parallel world I would always wish myself to be a part of, crouched by one broad and brimming tractor-rut on the farm track near our house in Chesham.

Standing now in the Sanctuary's circle, I remember a panel in the Avebury museum: something about the underworld, that the stones were perhaps in contact with an underworld realm where the dead rested or roamed. What if the descending mirror-self of the hill was imitating that movement, and that movement, that descent, was connected to a Neolithic vision of the past in which the dead were still alive, both real and unreal – both exactly as they were and mere wraiths that the slightest breeze could ruffle and make vanish?

And might that not make the shimmering water's surface a precise enactment of the present?

Past, present, future, for a people who did not really conceive of time.

At the age of nineteen, I was invited through a friend, whose father was a leading archaeologist, to join a dig on an important Neanderthal site in Jersey, a coastal ravine that served as a hunting shelter from 238,000 BC to as recently as 40,000 BC, when it was occupied by some of the last surviving Neanderthals. We camped on the heathery common behind, a vertiginous climb away, and sat around a big open fire in the evenings: it was so cold at night that I hardly slept, but I was in my element.

The cave would have commanded a gully-fissured landscape now concealed by the English Channel, roamed by mammoth, deer, rhino, wild horses and wolves – there was extreme climate change over such a long period of (albeit broken) occupation, but the air was generally a lot colder. I was assigned the hearth, which I had to picture as a long unbroken column of ash. The column, from which I picked carbonised twigs, a hefty greenstone hand axe and two spear points – one flint, one quartz – continued down in precisely the same spot for thousands of years, each dark inch burrowing through the silt of countless centuries and showing what archaeologists rather dully term 'fire management'.

I remember my trowel striking something hard, the axe's bulk growing through the damp sediment until it was finally seeing sunlight for the first time in some 135,000 years: the last eye to settle on it, the last hand to cradle it as mine was doing, did not belong to *Homo sapiens sapiens*, but to a species of human with a bigger brow ridge, no chin, and a larger jaw, who clustered in tiny groups of about five or six in a relatively unpopulated world and suffered as a result from serious in-breeding... yet I felt as if the owner of this wondrous tool was whispering to me. The 5,000 years of recorded history – since Sumer, or the first pyramids, or Silbury Hill – shrivelled into insignificance. It was a profound moment of internal readjustment that has never left me.

1976 feels a long time ago, nevertheless: some two decades later, in a kind of trance, I wrote a sequence of poems, *From the Neanderthal* – in the sense of 'from' another language – and this became the title poem of my third collection; very recent research on fossilised bone from a Neanderthal's vocal tract suggests that their language may have been as sophisticated as modern humans, so I wasn't so askew. On the off-chance that 'my' hand-axe might be identifiable, I wrote to the Jersey Museum Service who managed to track down the tool to a display in Guernsey Museum. They took a photograph and I was reunited, at least visually, with my find. It made a suitable book-cover, as the greenstone shapes a face, eerily like the oldest known portrait of a woman, from Dolni Vestonice in Moravia. Carved from mammoth ivory, it was created some 100,000 years after the hand-axe: both are long and elegant and hollow-eyed, like a simplified Modigliani face. A mournful spirit of the stone, or an involuntary reflection?

> The shrubs are gathering in
> their signs and symbols:
> it is winter again.
>
> So frail, the summer,
> I would like to plait it
> like grass, and keep my place
>
> in the book of my life
> forever, now, here.
> I've noticed this is not possible.
>
> Something is always ushering us.

Half an hour ago – an infinitesimal sliver – I was being drummed across the field by Kim and Robin. Time is not what my watch says (although it is growing so dark that I can't read it properly, and I don't have a mobile), but a distance, the long strides between myself as I stand here and the drumming, the field's tussocks, that surprising sense of being cared for. Distance, shape, solidity: time as a bowl-like space to be filled with memory and with what I do not remember. The white blank of oblivion replacing the fullness of what happened, much like a Rachel Whiteread sculpture, her casts of the interiors of rooms, turning them into monumental blocks no one can enter. A stick moving downstream, jerkily and then rapidly and then spinning slowly in an eddy. It is there and then it is here, in this moment of deep dusk.

What if, once upon a time, we experienced Einstein's spacetime – the theory of special relativity – as something more actual and immediate than abstract calculation? 'Space and duration are one,' wrote Edgar Allan Poe in his long prose-poem, *Eureka* (1848): purely intuitively, of course. (What Poe considered his greatest work is still dismissed by critics as an absurdity – although Einstein thought it 'very beautiful'.) Silbury is not some minutes' walk away but that walk itself away. It must all have been coded in the expression, in how they spoke it. How prehistory spoke: that is what we have lost.

Surprisingly, I am alone. The Ridgeway café in the gravel car park over the road has long been pulled down, if only to lessen the dangers of one of the nastiest road-crossings anywhere: right on the brow of the hill on a blind bend round which cars and lorries still ominously hurtle. The Sanctuary is just that: a sanctuary, although no longer a room. For it began life around 3000 BC as a circular hut, with an outer wall of eight oak posts and a central post for the thatched roof. Another much larger hut was built around it a couple of hundred years later, this in turn dwarfed by a third hut with three concentric rings of posts, one of which incorporated sarsen stones.

Aubrey Burl reckons these huts to have been charnel-houses for the dead, the rituals connected to the process of decay – citing practices among the Virginian Indians and in the New Hebrides. Dozens of part-scorched human bones have been unearthed here, along with the remains of feasting. The huts were eventually surrounded by a boundary-like circle of forty-two stones, 138 feet in diameter, and linked to the contemporary stone circle at Avebury by a processional line of sarsens – the Kennet Avenue. Thus it remained, more or less, until Farmer Green. And I try to recycle all these facts as the concrete markers fade to vague blobs, but what is more important is the cool breeze starting to blow and whether I will see my way up to the West Kennet Long Barrow without a torch, because the present is never still.

Silbury is a black manifest against the last of the light.

The track up to the long barrow's high ridge from the A4 is pale enough to stand out in the quickening darkness. Kim said that folk would be gathering here towards midnight, a modern tradition, summoning the dead spirits or just imbibing the vibes off this long wedge of burial mound in otherwise featureless ploughland: it converts even the least suggestible visitor. From the track, its 350 feet stretch out along the ridge as if some furry species of serpent is lying in wait, mouth filled with a curved array of sarsen teeth. For 1,000 years, between 3500 BC and 2500 BC, locals brought their kith and kin here to be entombed. Like Silbury, it would have been chalk-white, a brilliant crest visible for miles around, like the first inklings of foam on a smooth breaker. White death against green life: the immediate woodland cleared for the clan's mausoleum.

Today its eeriness is heightened by the fact that I am alone and it is almost dark; the sky is a wash of indigo blue in which the Pole star shines frostily, while the sepulchral serpent, silhouetted blackly against that sky and so making it a shade lighter, seems to have a beating heart.

A muffled boom, boom, boom.

As I approach the slabbed forecourt, dim and confusing in the twilight, there's a scuffle of feet and the drumming heartbeat stops. I circle the barrow for a few moments, its length like an inky mountain range against the deepening blue, struck more than ever by its immensity. The tump of Silbury sits clear and black in the distance, beyond the thrusting verticals of the sarsens that guard the entrance. Then I go in, finding the hip-wide slit between them by its flickery glow. As usual my ears feel tamped, as if entering an anechoic chamber: no wonder the drum sounded muffled. I once heard a girl on a stalled train shout down her mobile, 'We are so not near London, mate, you wouldn't believe it!' Well, you are so not outside in here, you wouldn't believe it.

There is a movement in the deepest cell, 42 feet in, and I advance gauchely. Thalamos. The inner chamber of a Greek house in ancient times: Homer repeatedly describes the bedroom of Paris and Helen in the *Iliad* as *thalamos*. This is what the long-haired woman with a stout candle has made of the long barrow, right in its far depths. Her own sanctuary. And here I am, crouched, awkward between the bulky stones, the chambers either side dressed in smaller beewsax candles dripping onto the sarsen ledges, my maleness never so evident to me as right now. She is dressed entirely in black, in a robe of black, and has very long silvery-white hair, although she is certainly younger than me. Ageless, perhaps. I spot the worry in her eyes as I stand up straight in the final circular chamber, so I smile goofily and say a very unNeolithic, 'Hi there'.

The round chamber is small and we fill it. I wonder briefly if she is a Satanist, rather than a straightforward pagan, as the barrow has long been a favourite with a variety of cults, as well as psychics, earth-healers, spiritual drummers and so on. Wodges of wax have collected on the ledges, along with the usual offerings: it even smells like a Catholic shrine. Thirty years ago I found in the depths what we called then a rubber johnny, whether used for ritualistic purposes or a simple quickie I have no idea, along with an empty bottle of beer: the place reeked of piss and damp.

It has always been a depot for our sweepings: when in use, it was piled to the ceiling with ritual objects, and bones were taken from the skeletons, presumably for use in ceremonies here or elsewhere. Slim bone-whistles were found, whistles having always been a favourite accessory for shamans everywhere. It is thought likely that the barrow's forecourt and the womb-like interior were, in fact, the scene of shamanic rituals, getting in touch with the ancestors, whistling up the spirit world – much like the forecourt of a Hindu temple, its candlelit interior flickering beyond the rite, the possessed dance of the gods. I'm finding that I don't want to stay in here: there's a sultry heaviness, a sense that I'm not wanted, a kind of torpid reluctance to welcome me in. Perhaps I'm just picking up the woman's thoughts.

Male power, female power. Standing stones and wooden posts like phallic sentinels, mounds like bellies with child, barrow interiors like wombs. Were there two spirit categories, too?

Fire, water.

The wax-scented heaviness is hardly surprising, since in the five chambers the remains of fifty individuals of various ages were found: some closely resembled each other, while all the adults showed signs of severe arthritis. The estimated five families belonging to the clan that built this enormous barrow, hauling up the usual tonnage of sarsens for the façade and walls and roof, would have struggled not only against dead weight but also against their own joint pain, let alone – among numerous other ailments – the distracting agony of tooth abscesses. The Neolithic and its drift towards agriculture brought new diseases and complaints, along with social hierarchies and copper axes for the elite and, eventually, war in the Bronze and Iron Ages and all the slivers of ages since.

I break the silence – it is embarrassing being so close without communicating – by saying how the candles make it look special. It's true: the flickering, darting shadows on the rock walls, the scent of beeswax and incense, have cancelled the damp sterility of a place disembowelled by archaeology, by our desire to know and to analyse. Sometimes I think that invasive archaeology is a metaphor for our whole current situation: the process of discovery necessitates destruction.

'They do, yes,' she said. 'Very peaceful.'

She gives a nervous chuckle, as English people do when feeling shy. Not very forthcoming, but neither am I. Words just seem to flop in here.

I move into the side-chamber along the passage; did she put the candles here too, or are these further mute offerings from those living over 5,000 years after the last body to be laid to rest? The barrow was in use, with the odd century-long pause, for a whole millennium… before being filled up with chalk rubble and broken pottery and then sealed by the two seven-ton sarsens that still block its broad entrance, through which you have to squeeze. Were the bones brought in only when clean of flesh, as in an ossuary (secondary burial, it is known as, practised in various parts of the world throughout prehistory), or did the tomb stink of rotting corpses?

There is such a contrast between the expansiveness of the downs outside and this deep, crouched interior!

Depression is like this. You can be somewhere wide open and wonderful and yet be trapped in a close darkness, within thick walls of stone. Was this underplace the realisation of what they thought death was, a state always entered alone? To enter it homeopathically, as it were, and thus see out of it to something post-mortem – an after-life? In trance? Was this dangerous? Was this playing with death, in some way? Or was it more pragmatic: a setting-apart of their kin that kept them close enough for reverence, visible yet still buried? A death-house with five bedrooms. In traditional African belief, myriad though its forms are, the horrible aloneness of death's journey out of a tribal togetherness is what is feared most of all.

When my teenage home was in Cameroon, I went with my family up north on a minibus tour into the Mandara mountains, where neat defensive huddles of sharply conical thatched huts encircled by mud walls dot the lunar mountains,

like something out of Tolkien – or the English Neolithic. The odd naked man or woman, blue-black and lean and elegant, worked the neat terraces under the gruelling sun with hoes

that had not changed for millennia. As the main character in
V. S. Naipaul's East African novel *In a Free State* caustically
puts it, 'The romantic blacks are the backward ones,' his
quasi-racist self-consciousness troubling his own deep love
for the continent. With less awareness, I assumed these
people had been here since time immemorial. In fact, they
were only living in this inhospitable country as the result of a
Fulani jihad in 1809, the pagan 'godless ones' fleeing to these
barren hills and cultivating every sparse inch of available soil
with a tact and sophistication that makes the technological
West look yobbish.

Each Kirdi village is self-ruling, creating what is effectively
a 'horizontal' society, although there is a chief in Oudjila, the
largest village, with limited powers. Our dusty vehicle bounced
into an area without any kind of modern amenity, and I was
aware, when we alighted, of the stink of our exhaust.

We visited His Majesty Mozogo Daouka in his *sare*, or
palace, a labyrinth of mud-walled cells and sloping paths
and a courtyard full of enormous cylinders which serve as
everything from storage to bedrooms. The chief's fifty wives
(and numerous children) leaned or sat against the dry-baked
mud of their individual rooms and eyed us as we were shown
around. The naked-breasted women in their elaborate beaded
jewellery looked on impassively, their ages ranging from
pubescent to wrinkled seniority. The chief – a strikingly tall
and muscular man with a grizzle of grey hair – informed us
that two of them would sleep with him each night, indicating
the wooden cupboard in which one or other had to wait
her turn (this intense activity must have done him good, as
at time of writing he is still alive, just short of a hundred,
still showing the tourists round). Here in his Hobbit-like

bedroom was the only sign of the twentieth century in the entire village: a yellowed newspaper photograph of the Queen visiting Yaoundé in the 1950s.

At the other end of the palace was the sacred bull, shuffling and glowering in its pitch-black compound – which was in effect another cell. Each year a two-year-old bull is placed here in the gloom, not seeing daylight until it is brought out to be ritually slaughtered at harvest-time. These mountain people are animists, as were the Apache – and most of humanity once upon a time: the bull is their totem, or even one of their gods. Animism is no less complex than Islam, which the area has successfully resisted for centuries. The chief pointed out where his father was buried: under what had once served him as his bed. I asked if anyone still used that room. 'Of course,' he laughed. 'Why not?'

Outside, ancestral skulls grinned from pots by the doors of the huts.

I was eighteen, still feeling immortal, and was struck by how healthy this approach to life and death was: better to have God in an animal or a tree than in the sky, perhaps, and better to keep your loved ones where you pass your days and nights, the veil almost transparent. The list of diseases and the low life expectancy of the Neolithic is part of this area's experience, too, but how envious I felt of this simpler, self-sufficient existence! And how normal it all was, somehow; as if the simplicity, the directness, was not, in fact, some romantic creation of my own but engraved in my ancestral memory, etched in the genes.

Perhaps once I would have found this true of West Kennet Long Barrow, but now I find it a confused deposit of desires and beliefs that both enliven and obscure its fundamental meaning: it is scribbled over. This, no doubt, is much truer to reality, perhaps even the Neolithic reality, where power squabbles and conflicting ceremonial customs and cattle raids and festering jealousies and contemporary types of jihad might have been the natural weave of things, for nothing stays still.

Outside, I am glad to be alone again: the barrow looms as a thicker darkness, with one horizontal slit of bright white light in the cloud-cover to the west, as if we are still in the sepulchre, still far from the opening. A fresh night breeze is blowing over the expanses of grass and ploughland. Within minutes the bright strip has turned a russet yellow, widening and fading, the barrow's contours against it simply another long horizon, both near and far, dying into darkness.

I stumble back on the very last dregs of the sunset, the absence of moon rendering the track periodically gully-like. Just beyond the metal gate about halfway down, I sense something racing towards me from below. I glimpse a little figure in animal hides, arms held forward above the head and holding up a kind of large cape as if sheltering under it – deerskin, it looks like, with pale speckles. The apparition rustles past me – it makes a strange sort of whispering or hissing sound as it runs – and so extraordinary a vision is this that I stop, seriously wondering if it isn't another time-slip, another Neolithic conjuring.

A few seconds later, I am disappointed to hear the solid click of the gate-latch. The surface has not broken after all.

In my fourth poetry collection, *Nine Lessons from the Dark*, I included a poem about West Kennet Long Barrow, called 'Neolithic'. It's actually about time and memory, because

I recall myself as a boy, a memory that itself feels as if it belongs to another time, another age – and yet which is continually present, like everything that's happened in history (and prehistory). Back in 2003, in a startling case of prolepsis, I anticipated that running, deer-skinned figure.

Here are four sections from the poem:

Neolithic (West Kennet Long Barrow, *c.* 3500 to 2500 BC)

1

We'd have done for them, anyway:
dope-heads, darkies, aboriginal scrum

of simpletons. Our home-grown gingery
version of the Apache, soon to become

gloom under stone, a litter of fags and condoms,
a forty-foot corridor of corbelled rock

rammed into Wiltshire and still, after all
these years, stiff under its jeans of downland.

2

For a rough ten hundred winters,
we know, they coughed around it, tending

their earthwork of slow-motion grief
in a running commentary of crows,

though silence comes off them like a smell.
Spina bifida twisted a few

of their spines, we can tell: a long insignia
of paralysis, a burr in the gods'

teasing of the wool. Of all their stories
(envy, murder, love, humiliation),

just one invented proper noun
and the stave-lines of absent adzes.

3

The mud's still shiny as gristle,
the trees blurred in the mist's daguerrotype

that shows me as a schoolboy, here,
alone, scraping, hoping for a find –

before the rich sods smashed my bicycle
and left it by the Chapel like a trophy.

4

After I found my bike done in
(its delicate Deralier gears contorted,

the broken chain coiled around the frame
in a double helix of greasy links,

the air fled from the tyres), I'd walk
to the barrows. It took more time,

though the time was mine. Anorak snapping
on the tombs like a cloak, I'd dream of kings,

the future sprawled like smoke or the corn
below. I did not know, I did not think

how history is mostly repair and revenge,
coming at us like the wind up there

on a winter morning: a dormitory
of bones and fear we'd thought far off,

dealt with, finished, long buried beneath.
But no, it's here and you're the guest

and ghost, antlered and drawn and running.

Eight

There is certainly fire, as promised, in the Avebury ceremony. It glows and sparkles and swoops about as we walk across the north-east arc to where the labyrinth is now a hive of activity.

My wife Jo and our old Marlborough friends Sasha and Ray have joined me. It is not even two hours since I was inside the long barrow, yet now I am with people I know and love and life feels lighter on the mind. Tiny wigwam-like structures pulse golden from within, fire-dancers juggle or spin brilliance around themselves with burning poi, paraffin lamps shine like white stars, while a plethora of glow sticks – a chemiluminescent blue or green – introduces a modern party note. Otherwise – in the gaps, as it were – it is very dark.

The drums sound rhythmically and flames flicker from a tripod-hung cauldron in the labyrinth's centre. A long and doleful queue has built up, each person having to endure a whispered rite of passage with a man pretending to be bent and ancient and disagreeable in a cloak and hood; he holds a large stick. Words erupt from him in a guttural snarl. 'Why?' 'What?' 'How?' 'Do you *mean* this?' 'Selfish!' 'You've jumped the queue!' 'Next!' Now and again he roars like a maniac, 'You may not come in!' and shakes the stick with great violence –

the reason for the refusal I cannot fathom, although I stand as close as I dare. 'You may walk around, but not come in!'

Someone in a Green Man cloak informs us that you walk the labyrinth to banish something negative from the last year, having written it down on a slip of paper – which you throw into the central cauldron when you reach it. If the 'Gatekeeper' feels you haven't thought hard enough about your negative thing, you are turned away. It is a ham performance, but its authentic seriousness makes it eerie, almost troubling. Even the Druidically-dressed can be refused; even those done up in animal skins with little leather pouches or long woollen robes like extras from *Excalibur* or *Lord of the Rings*. Even those with magnificent long beards. Only one person, a large woman under a bonnet, objects – and is shouted at ferociously.

Jo suggests I give it a go, as I have had a pretty negative year, but the idea of being refused puts me off. The reward of entry is to walk the labyrinth slowly, holding a short lurid-green glow stick; it reminds me of shuffling towards security in crowded airports. I know, of course, that if I were to succeed in entering, I would be feeling quite differently: rituals work best for those undertaking them. We are spectators, out of the force field. It's like hearing a film through the cinema doors.

This is not Theyyam, not that god-thumped glowing mound. Nevertheless, the shuffling figures look authentically melancholic, bearing marks of woe: a slow meandering of negative thoughts – someone ill, a death, a divorce, a bully at work – creates a vortex that plunges away in the middle. It all makes a tense contrast with the fire-dancing, the drumming and whooping and general rattle-shaking going on around the edge and off towards the stones.

We circle the labyrinth's perimeter. The burning charcoal smell, the odd figure in stitched-hide dress crouched over a steaming pot, help to persuade that this is about as close as one can ever get, in England at least, to experiencing what might have happened in the stone circles when they were functioning. The crucial element is the sweaty atmosphere of belief: this is not an English Heritage recreation. These people, however hammily theatrical the whole business seems, are dead serious; just as Holy Communion in the politest of Anglican churches is dead serious with its potent words, its sweet whiffs of wine, its murmurings at the altar rail, its ritual cleansing of negativity.

In the mid-1980s, when I was a full-blown mime artist in London and teaching 'physical theatre' at an ILEA sixth-form college in the East End, we took our students to the windmill at Burnham Overy Staithe on the north Norfolk coast for a five-day workshop. For some, this was the first time they had left London, let alone seen the countryside. My course was entitled 'Ritual', an extension of my lessons on the origins of theatre – a natural subject for mimes, I suppose. The group was split into two, teachers included, and each on successive evenings had to put the others through a homegrown ceremony involving the four elements.

I will never forget what these Eastender kids achieved: it was a profound experience, being taken through a natural ritual without any technological effects apart from battery-powered torches. Approaching through darkness to see figures waving green branches up on the windmill's gallery, half-man, half-tree; the trickle of water into a bowl; whisperings and hummings; the smell and touch of seaweed and moss when blindfolded; gifts of sand-smoothed pebbles and shells; the touch of comforting hands; the flicker of flame throwing immense shadows; overlapping voices murmuring spells and votive honourings to nature... If this was powerful, what might it have felt like when the world was thick with spirits that needed to be appeased? When the stage was not a National Trust windmill but an unimaginably vast ring of stones concealed behind a high wall of chalk, or atop a great white hill floating in water?

I notice something extraordinary, suddenly.

Passing the one great sarsen still upright in the stripped north-east sector – stone 201, a lone sentinel from the inner circle – I notice how the fire-play is sending shadows dancing over the stone's broad flank. Human shadow-figures weave in and out, larger and smaller depending on their distance from the light-source, which itself is ever-changing. I am amazed: it is like an art-film, a projection using backlighting and superimposition and foreground fade-out and diffusers and dissolve.

The stone lends itself peculiarly well as a screen, being pale and flat and smooth, apart from two horizontal gouges that move as the light moves and turns the stone to something alive, rippling and febrile and alive.

I stare transfixed: why has no one realised this before?

But they have. Thomas Hardy noticed when passing the 'Druid Stone' in his garden. Tormented by guilt and grief after the death of his wife, Emma, he 'stopped and looked at the shifting shadows/That at some moments fall thereon/From the tree hard by with a rhythmic swing,' and imagined them shaping to 'the shade that a well-known head and shoulders/Threw there when she was gardening.' Here, in 'The Shadow

on the Stone' (1917), we have the elision of shadow and ghost, a simple physical occurrence converted by the poet's haunted imagination to the status of a revenant. The actual stone had nothing to do with the Druids – although Hardy believed it had and that it had magical properties – but was part of a Neolithic circle or burial site.

Revenants.

Imagine the procession down Avebury's two avenues: even the most level-headed scholar thinks it probable that fire and dancing would have been integral to any ceremonial rite in here: think of all the folk interpretations of erected stones as frozen dancers. I give a voice to a stone circle in my poem *The Nine Ladies on Stanton Moor*:

> Cromlechs rise routinely from mists:
> we are granite lumps. We know
> how ugly we are, and once how lovely.

The ladies were turned to granite for dancing to a fiddle on the Sabbath, the fiddler suffering the same fate forty yards off. Set amidst Scots pines on a moor thick with Bronze Age remains near Bakewell in Derbyshire, my father's native county, this beautiful circle has long been a favourite with pagan groups: I once approached it at nightfall in the early 1980s to find a fire lit in the middle and flesh-and-blood dancers boogying to drums, the shadows swirling over the tussocks like the spokes of a wheel.

The Avebury avenues' stones would have served as natural screens, their flattish sides creating a parallel shadow-realm in which the shamans or priests reared and pranced and grew suddenly enormous, endlessly shape-shifting, the stones glowing and pulsating as the projected flame-light struck.

Theatrical, as all rituals are in part.

And worryingly impressive, even terrifying, to anyone with evil designs on the clan or tribe.

How did the prehistoric mind interpret the casting of shadows? Not as a physical process of blocked light rays, obviously, but perhaps as a poiesis of spirit, the subtle body escaping the flesh, the revelation of the mysterious thisness that survives death and dissolution.

This is what strikes me, watching the complex shadow-dance on the great solitary stone in the north-east sector: like a child not yet tutored in a world stripped of metaphor, I see it as a capturing, not a projection. A kind of X-ray of whatever spirit-skeleton lies inside us. And now this spirit has become other, somehow – independent, freed, shape-shifting. The dance of the dead who are also alive. The veil between ripped.

It must be the drumming that's encouraging this trance-like suspension of disbelief: I have certainly not imbibed of any suspect substances. It is simply the power of the image, moving as I have seen the Uffington White Horse move under a full moon scudded over by swift clouds; as the painted Palaeolithic animals moved and rippled under the firelight of torches on the uneven cave-rock.

The Ice Age Art exhibition in the British Museum had examples of presumed shadow puppets tens of thousands of years old: one unique male figure in ivory had articulated limbs, with neat holes for cords or rods and a prominent nipple and genitals. It would have been able to dance, looming enormous as the puppeteer (quite possibly a shaman) held it closer to the firelight. This is my shadow, my spirit, look, it leaves my body and can fly. Just as the spirits of the dead can fly, called up by charms, prancing and swooping. The mumbled litany, the close tent or cave, the incipient fear and wonder.

Puppets, whether shadow or real, have formidable power to cast a spell, to entrance. My favourite puppet in my performing days was made of sponge, a rod puppet with a big mouth called Percy. He took over when I played him, so lifelike that I just let him speak. My grown-up children are still seriously nervous of him whenever I open the suitcase and take him out of moth-eaten retirement.

Shadows and puppets. Half in, half out. Thresholds. Liminality. Flesh and spirit overlapping and separating: good medicine, but dangerous. The Avebury stones may have – no, they would have, their broader facets facing inwards, their bulges and hollows and flatnesses – enhanced and captured all this visual magic. Shadows must have been a central element to prehistoric lives. Making animal silhouettes from your bare hands is something we learn as children: in a world of natural, uncertain light and much more darkness, this would have been a primary imaginative impulse – after (as the experts explain it) the pre-frontal cortex had developed its full capacity around 50,000 years ago. The same BM exhibition showed what may have been small mobiles (including a flying duck, ironically) that would have created complex shadows on the cave wall as they moved or spun in cave draughts.

In 2013, Jean Jacques Lefrère and Bertrand David – neither of them prehistorians – suggested in their book *La plus vieille énigme de l'Humanité* that the famous 'realistic' cave paintings of Lascaux, Chauvet and other cave sites, seen as among the first ever art works and of an astonishing level of accomplishment, were created with the help of silhouettes thrown by small carvings of animals (similar to some recovered artefacts) placed in front of an oil lamp. The authors point out that most of the horses, aurochs, mammoths or whatever are in profile, look very similar, and many lack eyes or other internal details – conforming to outline drawings. They frequently overlap each other, creating a mass of animals of different sizes that would be very hard to draw without some sort of guide.

This does nothing to diminish the skills of the painters, of course (art has always had an element of the ingenious and pragmatic), as what they then did to convert the bare outline into a mimesis of a living beast is just as extraordinary: as Picasso remarked, on emerging from Lascaux, 'We have discovered nothing!' (Chauvet's paintings have been dated to *c.* 34,000 BC). But it does suggest that we have underestimated the importance of the play of light and shadow – exactly the elements that no archaeologist will ever recover, as nothing could be more ephemeral. Like spoken words themselves.

Shadows shift their length not only depending on the time of day, but on the time of year: at southern Britain's latitude, at midday on the winter solstice, a person's shadow is roughly four times their height; this shrinks by half on the summer solstice. The great French cinematographer Henri Akelan, who started work as a travelling puppeteer before being hired as a cameraman, was a master of light and shadow: the films he worked on include masterpieces like Marcel Carné's *Quai des Brumes*, Jean Cocteau's *La Belle et la Bête* and Wim Wenders' *Wings of Desire*. In his remarkable book *Des lumières et des ombres*, explaining his life's work, he distinguishes between ordinary daylight, whose regularity situates us in 'space-time' (and whose fading at twilight has long caused us dread), and the shadows created by that light, each shadow holding a 'balance of power' with the object casting it: the greater the shadow, the more minimal the object becomes in comparison, and vice-versa. We see this not only in film but in the paintings of masters like Georges de la Tour, Caravaggio, Goya, Rembrandt or Joseph Wright of Derby. Akelan goes on (my translation):

> An object's real dimensions are affected by the relationship it maintains with its shadow; it takes on an imaginary dimension. Whence the importance of the power of shadows, acting upon our judgement by making us briefly perceive as large what is small, as diminished what is monumental, as fabulous what is ordinary, as exceptional what is banal. It is through shadow-play that the uncanny is suggested – a combination of reality and illusion... of the palpable and the impalpable.

Ordinary sunlight does not appear to move, unless flecked by shifting leaves in a wood. Flame-light – candle, torch or blazing fire – is an 'artificial' light that moves ceaselessly; Akelan points out that, not only is such light a statement of human power and control in a bewilderingly diffident universe, but that its unsettled, unsteady quality 'conjures complex feelings, mixing the precise and the imprecise, what is designated and what is unexpressed...' The irrational, in other words. A hidden world. This is what I felt on watching the shadow-play on the great sarsen stone: this is what I feel on watching a Hitchcock film and its psycho-physical blurrings or, a touch more lyrically, *La Belle et la Bête*.

What has come down to us as picturesque ruin, as melancholy reminder of human transience, as haunting relic of an ungraspable ancientness, might instead be regarded, with a breath of informed imagination, as something quite other, trackable like a deer's slots in snow to what is utterly modern: as something that might have found its place (had we the evidence) in the history of what is known as 'pre-cinema' – with a trace of that intensity, that prehistoric reverence, awe and even fear, surviving in the familiar spell cast by a darkening auditorium.

That night in bed, mind racing from my few hours in the parallel country of pagan enchantment that has never really gone away – like a guardian of the island's damaged fabric – I picture Silbury's great chalk-white hulk as it was back then, as sometimes we can glimpse it now when the grass is covered by snow.

If a person, whether antlered shaman or something quite other, were to place themselves (perhaps using a timber platform over the flooded ditch) between the hill's sloped flank and a correctly-positioned fire in the depths of night, and then approach the fiery, unsteady light-source, their figure would loom and stretch up the white blank of the hill: if many dancing figures were to join in, the spectacle would be breathtaking, and reflected in the flooded ditch beneath. The human individual would fall away like a shed skin and become god-like: that essence or spirit would grow to grandeur as each single shadow curved and split and coalesced and loomed up towards the sky, and deepen as its twin descended into the blurred underworld below, the surface of the present glittering with flame as the moments burn away and vanish.

A performance in the round. Water transfigured by flame in the usual fantastical alchemy. Fires spaced as they were spaced around that Wiccan labyrinth, burning like jewels in a great ring, the shadow-dance visible from wherever you squatted. Faces looking up, agape.

In 1914, R. Hippisley Cox, in *The Green Roads of England*, conjectured that 'Silbury, like the Pyramids of Egypt, was built as a great shadow hill to mark the progress of the sun', its pole on the summit establishing 'the proper seasons for seed-time and harvest': a more pragmatic version of Michael Dames's harvest hill. What if Silbury was indeed a Shadow Hill – but designed, not to cast shadows, but to capture them? The great shadow-spirits pressing themselves like thumbs into a pot's fresh clay… pressing and then sliding, shifting, to be impressed anew. Restless, as spirits and ghosts always are. For the firelight's brief term.

Of course this wasn't conceived of when the first basket-load of gravel was emptied, the first mud tumps patted into shape; but ingenuity and accident and maybe a dose of genius might have played their part as the hill rose whitely and the springs' water trickled into the ditch.

Perhaps nothing as spectacular and lovely has ever been created since on our islands – no work of art or architecture or technological achievement – and what we have now is the mere husk.

And yet even this husk is extraordinary: a relic reduced to pure form, onto whose grassy sides the shadows of our own imaginings are still projected and absorbed for as long as we are still around, stumbling and sometimes dancing through life towards unknown realms of darkness.

On Silbury Hill

1

I'm slogging up through cow-muck once again,
flanked by tussocks and the crumbly sores of burrows.

It's artificial and there's nothing at the core –
no tomb, no gold, no secret god lying in his pots.

The slog; this moment; and memory. And love
as crisp as the air is now, if you're lucky.

2

The locals would placate it with thick fig cakes
and sugared water – though I doubt that

satisfied this mother of a belly (or suckled
breast, or gargantuan eye) with its sallow-

haunted spring at Swallowhead, quadrilled
by the OS map to something pear-shaped, dead.

3

The pivot of it all, you feel, when up
on top – though life through this early mist's

more heard than seen: chain-saws, tractors,
the cracks of a gun. No birds from the corn.

At night, of course, it's the stadium glare
of the new, executive estates; a havoc

of headlights on the A4; the marigold
smudge of Swindon foxing the stars.

4

A dag-lock of wool on a low thorn
where the peak is sinking into itself,

like a whirlpool, like a plug's been pulled
on the magic of the earth. Though perched

on this swelling, an unlikely nipple, you can think
of it all out there as down the shit chute. No –

as cultic, odd; a rite, a god. To which
we're proffering, not what they've found

in here (turf, antler-picks, a rusted bridle-bit)
but lands and seas and skies, and all their life.

Select Bibliography

A full list of those books which have influenced my thoughts about Silbury and the chalklands in general would be never–ending; the following is a list of works either cited in the monograph or which have been especially useful and inspiring. There are numerous websites devoted to the subject of megalithic monuments, in all shades from the academic to the eerie, and YouTube offers a generous selection of documentary films and amateur clips, ranging from a view deep inside the mound via a remote visual inspection system, to Derek Jarman's early Super-8 short, *A Journey to Avebury* (1971), in which Silbury is conspicuously absent.

Ackroyd, Peter, *Thames: Sacred River* (Chatto & Windus, 2007)

Akelan, Henri, *Des lumières et des ombres* (Editions du Collectionneur, 1984)

Aubrey, John, *Monumenta Britannica* (1626–97), ed. John Fowles (1980)

Betjeman, John, *Summoned by Bells* (Murray, 1960)

Bocquet–Appel, Jean–Pierre, and Tuffreau, Alain, 'Technological Responses of Neanderthals to Macroclimatic Variations, 240,000–40,000 BC', *Human Biology* Vol. 81, No. 2/3

Brentnall, H.C., 'The Marlborough Castle Mound', *Wiltshire Archaeological and Natural History Magazine* Vol 87, p.112

Burkitt, M.C., *Our Early Ancestors* (Cambridge University Press, 2012)

Burl, Aubrey, *Prehistoric Avebury* (Yale, 1979)

Callow, P., and J.M. Cornford, *La Cotte du St Brelade 1961–1978: Excavations by C.B.M. Mc Burney* (Geo Books, 1986)

Canti, M.G., G. Campbell, D. Robinson and M. Robinson, 'Site Formation, Preservation and Remedial Measures at Silbury Hill' (CfA Rep 61/2004)

Chippindale, Christopher, *Stonehenge Complete* (Thames & Hudson, 1983)

Colt Hoare, Sir Richard, *The Ancient History of Wiltshire*, Vol 2 (1821)

Critchlow, Keith, *Time Stands Still* (Gordon Fraser, 1979)

Dames, Michael, *The Silbury Treasure* (Thames & Hudson, 1976)

Defoe, Daniel, *A Tour through the Whole Island of Great Britain* (1724–6)

Duck, Stephen, *Description of a journey to Marlborough* (1738)

Eliot, T.S., *The Waste Land and other poems* (1940; Faber & Faber, 2002)

Field, David, 'Great Sites', *British Archaeology*, Issue 70, 2003

Fleckinger, Angelica, *Ötzi, the Iceman* (Folio Vienna/Bolzano, 2011)

Gilpin, William, *Observations on the River Wye* (1782)

Golding, William, *A Moving Target* (Faber and Faber, 1982)

——————— *The Inheritors* (Faber and Faber, 1955)

Hall, Michael, *Harrison Birtwistle* (Robson, 1984)

Harris, Alexandra, *Romantic Moderns* (Thames & Hudson, 2010)

Herodotus, *Histories* 1.17–18; tr. Aubrey de Selincourt (Penguin, 1954)

Hill, Geoffrey, *Mercian Hymns* (Faber and Faber, 1971)

Hippisley Cox, Robert, *The Green Roads of England* (1914: The Lost Library, 2010)

Hopkins, Gerard Manley, *Poems and Prose* (1918; Penguin, 2008)

Hudson, W. H., *Nature in Downland* (Longman, 1900)

Jefferies, Richard, *The Hills and the Vale* (Oxford University Press, 1980)

Johnstone, Keith, *Impro: Improvisation and the Theatre* (Faber & Faber, 1979)

Jung, Carl, and Richard I. Evans, *Conversations with Carl Jung and reactions from Ernest Jones* (Van Nostrand, 1964)

Knight, Charles, *Old England: a pictorial museum of regal, ecclesiastical, municipal, baronial and popular antiquities* (1845)

Lamont, Richard, D.A., 'A comparative study of Lady Hertford's grotto at Marlborough and William Kent's illustration of Spring in James Thomson's *The Seasons*' (Master's essay, University of Oxford, 2013)

Lawrence, D. H., *Selected Poems* (Penguin, 2008)

Leary, Jim, and David Field, *The Story of Silbury Hill* (English Heritage, 2010)

Leary, Jim, M. Canti, D. Field, et al, 'The Marlborough Mound, Wiltshire. A further Neolithic Monumental Mound by the River Kennet', *Proceedings of the Prehistoric Society*, Vol. 79, December 2013

Lefrère, Jean Jacques, and Bertrand David, *La plus vieille énigme de l'Humanité* (Paris: 2013)

Lippard, Lucy, *Overlay: Contemporary Art and the Art of Prehistory* (New Press, 1983)

Lorca, Federico Garcia, *Collected Poems* (1941; Pan MacMillan, 2002)

Macfarlane, Robert, *The Old Ways: A Journey on Foot* (Hamish Hamilton, 2012)

Mann, Nicholas R., *Avebury Cosmos* (O Books, 2011)

Marshall, Steve, 'Silbury Spring', *British Archaeology*, July–August 2013

Marshall, Steve, George Currie and Pete Glastonbury, 'Investigation of a "Sun Roll" Effect in Relation to Silbury Hill', *Time and Mind*, Vol. 3, Issue 3, Nov 2010

Massingham, H.J., *English Downland* (Batsford, 1936)

Naipaul, V.S., *In a Free State* (1971; Picador, 2011)

———————— *The Enigma of Arrival* (1987; Picador, 2011)

Oliver, Neil, *A History Of Ancient Britain* (Weidenfeld & Nicolson, 2011)

Orwell, George, *Why I Write* (1946; Penguin, 2004)

Osborn, George, and Rodney Legg, *Exploring Ancient Wiltshire* (Dorset Publishing, 1982)

Parker Pearson, Mike, *Stonehenge Riverside Project, Stonehenge* (Simon & Schuster, 2012)

Pitts, Mike, 'Excavating the Sanctuary: New Investigations on Overton Hill, Avebury', *Wiltshire Archaeological & Natural History Magazine* 94, 2001

Poe, Edgar Allan, *Eureka* (New York: 1848)

Pollard, Joshua, *Neolithic Britain* (Shire Publications, 2002)

Prior, F., *Britain BC: Life in Britain and Ireland Before the Romans* (Harper, 2004)

Rackham, Oliver, *The History of the Countryside* (Weidenfeld & Nicholson, 1986)

Serjeantson, Dale, 'Review of Animal Remains from the Neolithic and Early Bronze Age of Southern Britain, 4000 BC – 1500 BC' (Research Department Report Series no. 29, English Heritage, 2011)

Sinclair, Iain, *London Orbital* (Granta, 2002)

Stukeley, William, *Abury, a Temple of the British Druids, with Some Others Described* (London, 1743)

Thomas, Edward, *The South Country* (1932; Little Toller, 2009)

Thomas, Julian, *Understanding the Neolithic* (2nd Edition, Routledge, 1999).

Thomas, Julian, and Alasdair Whittle, 'Anatomy of a Tomb: West Kennet Revisited', *Oxford Journal of Archaeology* 5, 129–56, 1986

Thorpe, Adam, *Ulverton* (1992; Vintage Classics, 2012)

———————— *Mornings in the Baltic* (Secker & Warburg, 1988)

———————— *From the Neanderthal* (Cape, 1999)

———————— *Nine Lessons from the Dark* (Cape, 2003)

———————— *Birds with a Broken Wing* (Cape, 2007)

Timlett, Rose and Tom Le Quesne, Riverside Tales, *Lessons for water management reform from three English rivers* (World Wildlife Fund, 2010)

Tudge, Colin, *Trees* (Allen Lane, 2005)

Tufnell, Ben (ed.), *Richard Long: Selected Statements & Interviews* (Haunch of Venison, 2007)

Valéry, Paul, *The Collected Works*, Vol. 1, trans. by David Paul (Princeton University Press, 1971)

Whittle, Alasdair, Sacred Mounds, *Holy Rings: Silbury Hill and the West Kennet Palisade Enclosures – A Later Neolithic Complex in North Wiltshire* (Oxbow, 1997)

Wells, H.G., *The Secret Places of the Heart* (Macmillan, 1922)

Wilson, Jean Moorcroft, *Charles Hamilton Sorley* (Cecil Woolf, 1985)

Illustrations

Frontispiece, title page, pages 8, 22, 44, 154 and 208 © Ray Ward
Page 11 *Silbury Hill surrounded by flood water and mist* © English
Heritage **Page 12** Harold St George Gray, *Silbury Hill viewed from
alongside the Kennet stream, just southwest of Avebury* © Alexander
Keiller Museum **Page 14** *Silbury Hill, Wiltshire; Conjectured to be a
Colossal Barrow* © Look and Learn/The Bridgeman Art Library
Page 20 *Café & Petrol Pumps at Silbury Hill* © English Heritage
Page 25 *Uffington White Horse and Dragon Hill* © Adrian Cooper
Page 27 William Stukeley, *Silbury Hill viewed from the south-west and
main road* and *A serpentine view of the Druid temple of Avebury (map
of Avebury stone rings and Silbury Hill)* **Page 29** Richard Long *Silbury
Hill* © Richard Long, courtesy of Tate **Page 35** Paul Nash *Landscape of
the Megaliths* © The estate of Paul Nash, courtesy of the Victoria and
Albert Museum **Page 47** *Richard Atkinson looking into the* 1849 *tunnel,
Silbury Hill* © Alexander Keiller Museum **Page 49** *The author in front
of 'A' House, Marlborough College, 1970* © Adam Thorpe
Page 51 (clockwise from left, 1958-61*): The author with ayah, Calcutta;
the author on the beach with brother, sister and mother in Brittany; the
author with his mother in Baalbeck, Lebanon; the author in the garden
in Calcutta with his father.* © Adam Thorpe **Page 52** *'A' House, c.1915*
Page 54 *The Mound beyond the 1960s dining hall* **Page 55** *College
dormitory, c.1915.* **Page 65** Henry Moore *Stonehenge XI* © Henry Moore
Foundation, courtesy of Tate **Page 66** *Fyfield Down* © Adrian Cooper
Page 70 *Memorial Hall, Marlborough College, c.*1925 **Page 81** Joe
Tilson, untitled from *Wessex Portfolio* © Joe Tilson, courtesy of Tate
Page 85 *Postcard from Léopoldville (Kinshasa) from the author's father to
grandmother, 1966* © Adam Thorpe **Page 86** *Cameroon Airlines quad-
prop, 1975* © Adam Thorpe **Pages 87 and 88** *From the balcony, Douala,
1973* and *Mount Cameroon across the Wouri estuary, c.1975* © Adam Thorpe

Acknowledgements

Many people have helped in various ways with this exploration, some without knowing it. I am extremely grateful to Zoe Swenson-Wright for her freely offered editorial comments, some of which have been absorbed by the text, and to Ray Ward, who has not only illustrated some of the chapter headings but dug up some of the obscurer archive images. I would also like to thank the following for their contributions: Paul Wright, David Way, Christopher Edwards, Karen Hewitt, Helen Bourner, John Woolrich, Peter Metcalfe, Elsa Delage, Lucy Luck, Chris Clarke, Simon McBurney, Charles Lock, Richard Wistreich, Hubert Duprat, Sasha Ward and Robin and Kim. A special thanks to my wife Jo for cheerily accepting this book's gradual conversion from a modest hump to something which dominated our personal landscape for far longer than expected. Thank you to Adrian Cooper at Little Toller for triggering the enterprise and for his patience as additional material kept coming.

A.T., Cévennes 2014

Little Toller **Monographs**

Our monograph series is dedicated to new writing attuned to the natural world and which celebrates the rich variety of the places we live in. We have asked a wide range of the very best writers and artists to choose a particular building, plant, animal, myth, person or landscape, and through this object of their fascination tell us wider stories about the British Isles.

The titles

In preparation

A postcard sent to Little Toller will ensure you are put on our mailing list and amongst the first to discover each new book as it appears in the series. You can also follow our latest news at **littletoller.co.uk** or visit our online magazine **theclearingonline.org** for new essays, short films and poetry.

LITTLE TOLLER BOOKS
Lower Dairy, Toller Fratrum, Dorset DT2 0EL